# Decorating on eBay

# Decorating on eBay

### Fast and Stylish—on a Budget

## BARBARA GUGGENHEIM

*Photography by Jim McHugh*

ReganBooks
*An Imprint of HarperCollinsPublishers*

This book contains advice and information relating to buying and selling products on eBay. All efforts have been made to assure the accuracy of the information contained in this book as of the date of publication. The publisher and the author disclaim liability for any outcomes that may occur as a result of applying the methods suggested in this book. This book is not authorized, sponsored, or endorsed by eBay Inc.

The eBay website and all information and fees regarding eBay are subject to change.

HarperCollins books may be purchased for educational, business, or sales promotional use. For information please write: Special Markets Department, HarperCollins Publishers Inc., 10 East 53rd Street, New York, NY 10022.

FIRST EDITION

*Designed by Joel Avirom and Jason Snyder*

*Design Assistant: Meghan Day Healey*

Printed on acid-free paper

Library of Congress Cataloging-in-Publication Data
Guggenheim, Barbara
  Decorating on eBay : fast & stylish—on a budget
 Barbara Guggenheim.—1st ed.
    p. cm.
  ISBN 0-06-076248-9 (alk. paper)
   1. Interior decoration 2. Internet auctions. 3. eBay (Firm) I. Title.

NK2113.G827 2005
381'.456454—dc22

2005042835

05 06 07 08 09 10 9 8 7 6 5 4 3 2 1

To my husband Bert Fields, who makes me feel that I can do anything I put my mind to— if only I'd focus. So, darling, I'm going to redo your office now.

# CONTENTS

# INTRODUCTION

A WHILE AGO, I bought a lot of things on eBay that I needed for our beach house (pottery, lamps, and rugs) and had great results. Not only did I get some unique and interesting objects, but I found the process to be a lot more fun than I expected. When I finished, I missed it. Furthermore, I was curious to know if it was possible to decorate an entire house—top to bottom—using eBay. With the help of KB Home, which provided a model home and a budget, I set out to try. In chronicling my experiences, my goal was and is to encourage other people like myself, who have neither enough time nor enough money to go the traditional route in decorating their homes, to explore this alternative.

Decorating on eBay has all the advantages and very little downside. It's quick, cheap, and offers endless variety. You can shop anytime you want, day or night. You can decide on a budget and stay within the range. It's like going to dozens of shops and flea markets all at once—without any of the aggravation. The fact is, you're not limited by your community; the world is available to you. If you live in Detroit and there's a vase you want in South Carolina, you can go for it. And best of all, you can be creative on your own terms. You can have a Moroccan palace in Chicago or a New England cottage in Montana. It's your fantasy, and you can get it on eBay.

# I. THE BEGINNING

# Getting My Feet Wet

"OH, MY GOD. It's the house I've always wanted." That's what I told my husband Bert when he surprised me with the beach cottage we'd been coveting for years. As delighted as I was that the house would finally be ours, the thought of decorating it was unnerving. I work a sixty-hour week and take care of a family, pets, and a house to boot. My head was barely above water. How was I going to find the extra time, not to mention the money, to fix up another house, even if it was my dream come true?

Make no mistake, there's nothing I would enjoy more than cruising antique shops, shopping centers, and design marts. But most of them are closed evenings and Sundays when I have free time. Sure, I could have gone to the mall and bought most of the things I needed in a few stops. But everything would have been new and wouldn't have had the character I wanted.

Luckily, I didn't have to start from scratch. The seller left some large pieces of furniture, but each had its own drawback. For example, a gorgeous antique pine cabinet was absolutely perfect for the long wall in the dining area. But what could I display on its forty running feet of plate racks? A glass-paned corner cupboard gave the guest room its character, but what could I put in it that would look great without breaking the bank? I could easily see myself spending months I didn't have searching for these things, not to mention the rugs, lamps, towels, and dozens of other less

3

glamorous objects I needed.

On my desk was a mountain of catalogs, and I was tempted to buy everything mail order. Sadly, I didn't even have time to go through them. Besides, it seemed that the spirit of our Nantucket–style beach cottage would be better served by trying to find at least *some* vintage objects. **What I wanted was charm, but could I find it cheap** and not turn the activity into a second job?

I turned, with serious trepidation, to eBay. I'd heard all kinds of horror stories about it, like paying for an object that never arrives, or it comes, but it's a fake. A friend, Scott Hobbs, had been buying on eBay for a while, and he was happy to bring me into the fold. He'd bought a square glass plate at a flea market, which he used whenever he made his special fig cake. One day it broke, and Scott went to pieces, too. He went on eBay, desperate, and typed in "square glass plate." Up came several, some of which looked like his broken plate; they were called "jadeite." Finally, he knew what he had. He started buying and now has boxes of jadeite stashed in his garage. Hearing his story, I decided to try.

Scrolling through eBay for the first time, **I found a mix of objects—new, old, antique, and vintage**—much as you see at flea markets. The difference was that going to the flea market meant getting up before dawn, braving the rain or cold and a complaining husband. And there was always the risk of returning home empty-handed.

I realized I could accomplish the same thing on eBay without any of the hassle. I could go online at home on a Sunday morning in my pajamas with a cup of coffee next to me, or at the office during my lunch break. (Did you know sixty-three minutes of the average worker's day is spent on the computer doing personal things?) Better yet, I could be bidding after work with a martini in hand. What is it they say about liquid courage?

I racked my brain until I came up with the idea of filling the shelves in the dining area
with white ironstone. I didn't want a lot of color, and, after all, what could be more "country"
than ironstone on pine? So I started bidding with a vengeance—bowls, plates, tureens, and
pitchers. One morning, up at six, I thought I'd check on some bids I'd left the night before.
My husband, walking by, looked over my shoulder. "Ironstone Mike" had bid on a serving
platter I wanted. "This is sheer malevolence," Bert bellowed. (Forgive his choice of words;
he's written a book on Shakespeare and gets a little stagy now and then.) "Didn't 'Ironstone
Mike' bid on the pitcher and washstand we wanted?" Now furious, Bert wanted me to send
him an e-mail warning that if he ever outbids us again, we'll bid against him for the rest of
his life. Instead, we raised our bid a healthy $50. Bert was determined, even if he had to pay
more than the serving platter was worth.

eBay for building collections...and finding handmade items...

One night Bert pointed to a blank wall. "An old ship painting would look good there; let's try eBay." I was pessimistic. As an art consultant, I'd looked but never found any interesting paintings on that site. Nevertheless, I went on eBay and did a search for "old ship painting." A handful came up, each more horrible than the one before. There was even one painted on velvet! One caught my husband's eye—a watercolor. I warned him that it wasn't old, but that didn't discourage him. I left a bid, got the painting, and had to laugh at the follow-up e-mail from the seller, "I'm so glad you won my painting. I just finished it last night." In the seller's mind, I guess, "old" described "ship" and not "painting."

In the end, eBay was the answer to my prayers. It compressed time; it was efficient and fun. To find everything I needed—the perfect fabrics, lamps, rugs, and particularly **the collectibles** (ironstone, lighthouses, and sock monkeys)—would have taken months or years searching through flea markets, antique shops, shows, and malls, and cost thousands of dollars in gas. On eBay, it took only a few weeks, and I was delighted with the results. I wrote an article on my experience, which *Architectural Digest* published. How many times had I fantasized about having my house in *Architectural Digest*? Well, now I had to laugh. My dream came true, and I did it for just a few thousand dollars.

If I could decorate my house on eBay and get into *Architectural Digest*, why can't you?

Particularly special to me are pillows my mother made by sewing on buttons bought on eBay.

Artic Wh

CORIAN

OWNER

# The Challenge:
# Can I or Can't I?

*"Have nothing in your houses
which you do not know to be useful
or believe to be beautiful."*

—William Morris, 1880

SOME PEOPLE CLIMB MOUNT EVEREST, others paraglide. Not me. My idea of a challenge was decorating an entire house on eBay. It had been so much fun buying tchotchkes for our beach house, I wanted to see if it was possible to do a whole house on eBay, stem to stern—tables and chairs to sheets, towels, and knickknacks.

I wanted to prove that wherever you live, whether it's an apartment in Manhattan or a beach cottage in the Florida Keys, you can decorate your home as if you'd spent many weeks and many dollars shopping in the world's biggest and most expensive design centers and markets. That's the genius of eBay.

This isn't a style book. I couldn't do one if I tried. I have neither the flair nor the unique vision it takes. Nor does this book unveil a signature style (I don't have one) or reveal my personal decorating secrets (I don't have any of those either—I crib from others). It's simply a chronicle of my journey and lessons I learned.

When I was ten years out of college, my apartment still looked like a student dorm. Later, when my building went co-op and most of my savings went to the mortgage, my dining area didn't have a stick of furniture in it for years. Sound familiar? Believe me, I know how easy it is to think, "I'll never be able to afford to decorate the way I want, so why bother?" Now, after experiencing eBay, I'm sure that anyone, with imagination and even the most minimal resources, can get great results decorating with eBay.

Because this was an experiment, the décor of the house is somewhat "unusual." **Rather than all the rooms having a single "look," they're all different.** I think of it as a collection of American rooms. I did this not only to see if it was possible to find objects in a number of different eras and idioms, but also because I think that's how people really live. Not everyone in a household shares the same aesthetics or interests. So, for an imaginary twelve-year-old girl who's interested in fashion and whose favorite colors are pink and purple, a '60s room with a shag rug seemed natural. I thought a nine-year-old boy might relate to camouflage fabrics, a gym locker, and airplane models. The tiki bar loft was designed for a grown-up dad with retro feelings for music and surfing. The Bahamian-style master bedroom is an elegant, quiet oasis for a couple, away from the rest of the family. The downstairs guest room, with its Adirondack-style furnishings, was put together to make guests feel as if they've been transported to a mountain retreat. Finally, the California kitchen and dining area and the cottage living room provide family and friends with a cozy place to sit, eat, and talk.

KB HOME
CREEKSIDE
SANTA CLARITA, CA

SECOND ... RAMING PLAN

SHEAR WALL SCHEDULE: LOWER FLOOR

KB HOME

# The Proposition:
# An Offer I Couldn't Refuse

TO TAKE ON THE CHALLENGE, I needed a house to decorate. Bruce Karatz, chairman and CEO of KB Home, one of our nation's biggest homebuilders, graciously offered me the use of a yet-to-be-built model home and a budget of $50,000 (which had to include the cost of objects, shipping, and transformation, such as painting furniture, upholstering, and framing). KB Home understands that most people buying new homes are stretched financially and are looking for fast and inexpensive ways to decorate.

The house is in a development in Valencia, California, about thirty miles north of Los Angeles. On my first trip there, the development was nothing more than a vast tract of empty land. It would take almost four months to put in the infrastructure and forty-five days to build the house. That gave me almost six months to buy everything on eBay.

Although it's only 2,044 square feet, the house has a marvelous spacious layout. It has a huge master suite, three other bedrooms, three baths, an upstairs loft, and an open area combining living and dining rooms and a kitchen.

The finished Valencia House

# WORKING WITH WHAT YOU HAVE

When you buy a house, you're often stuck working with what you have—tiles, flooring, and kitchen cabinets. If you're gutting or building your own home you get to start from scratch. On eBay, you can find an array of structural items, from vintage sinks and cast iron radiators to new gas-fired boilers and Jacuzzis. There are several things to keep in mind:

- There's always the need for expertise. How do you know that the sink will thread into the pipes in your home? How will you install it?

- Where you live affects what you need to buy on eBay. For example, if you live near an outlet for old sinks and tubs, you might try looking there. Shipping costs of heavy items could outweigh what you're saving on the purchase.

- eBay has taken all the aces out of a deck of cards for you. Rather than go through numerous catalogs looking for what you want, eBay has grouped similar items together.

- Weigh time spent versus money saved. If searching out an old sink in shops that sell architectural castoffs would take too much time, then eBay makes sense. If you don't mind reproductions, a stop at Restoration Hardware may be better than waiting for the right ones to come up on eBay.

I picked the basics—flooring, dining room chandelier, bathroom and kitchen fixtures, and cabinetry—at a KB Home Studio, a giant sales facility (like a Home Depot). KB Home supplied beds as well.

# Setting the Stage

WHEN YOU DECORATE YOUR HOUSE, there's a lot of pressure to make a personal statement. The heat's on to reveal your sense of style and taste to the world. Most of us, when we're single, make do with furniture we got from our parents or, when married, we combine the stuff each of us had before. At a certain point, it's natural to want to step up and make our homes and apartments something special. Most of us could like a lot of styles and go in a number of design directions. It's easy to be overwhelmed by the process and sheer magnitude of choices available. I know—I was.

I started at a bookstore and library, buying and borrowing style and design books. Looking at photos of interiors, whether it's cottage-style, Shaker furniture, or Moroccan tiles, is as transporting for me as reading recipes must be to a foodie. I also bought a couple of months' worth of shelter magazines at a newsstand. That way, I could rip out pages without hesitation and put them in files, each labeled with a room in the house.

Cruising design centers, antique shops, fabric stores, and specialty stores like Pottery Barn and Crate & Barrel also gave me ideas. Since I had to buy all the furniture before the house was built, walking through sample rooms in shops and department stores gave me a better sense of what to expect in terms of space.

## my eBay way of decorating...

Hanky Hall

Bron's Room

Living room

Gire's Roo

...ny Room

Kids' Bath

Living r...

Bought
✓ green pots
✓ dried hyd...
✓ star fish
✓ ...een s...
✓ ...ies
✓ Arts ...alts fabric

CAMPAD

new, looking old

PAINT SCHEDULE — SHERWIN WILLIAMS
- GUEST BEDROOM
  SW6172
  COMPOSED
- ACCENT/TRIM — SW7005
  PURE WHITE

THE LURE OF THE WILDERNESS

Guest Bedroom
Adirondack Theme
collections:
    Navajo rugs
    Pendleton blankets
    sock monkeys
    fishing stuff
    decoys
to search
    fishing poles
    mattress fishing
    headboard
    decoys
    sock monkeys
    bark stuff
    Natl. Geographic

One rainy day, I took the files, room by room, disassembled them, and pinned the photos and articles on a corkboard. I called these my **inspiration boards.** As time went on, I added paint sample cards and anything else I found that I thought might be useful. Like a filmmaker, I was making a storyboard for each room. Then taking a set of ground plans, I drew in possible furniture layouts.

make lists of things to buy...

Finally, I was ready to browse on eBay. I chose "fabrics" first. I was excited to find a gorgeous piece of Ralph Lauren chintz (three yards)—roses against a blue-and-white striped background. There'd been only five bids, with only four hours and thirty minutes left. "Come look at the screen," I beckoned to my mother, who was visiting. "It'd make a great cushion for the alcove in the living room!" She leaned over, checked the yardage, and pulled back as if I'd committed the crime of the century. "My dear, haven't I taught you anything? The only way this will fit that cushion you have in mind is with the stripes going across, and horizontal stripes, darling, are just not done." I made a quick calculation. I could always use it for a small throw pillow, so I left a bid anyway. An hour later, I checked; someone had outbid me. I wondered, if I e-mailed him my mother's dictum about stripes, would he be deterred from further bidding? Instead, I panicked and doubled his bid; I had to have it.

At the time, I couldn't lose; it was only a few dollars. But what would happen when I had to find fabric for an important piece of furniture, such as the daybed I wanted in the master bedroom? If I had no confidence, how could I make the quick and canny moves to prevent other bidders from getting fabrics I wanted? A visit to a fabric store seemed like a good idea, so I spent an afternoon with Jason Asch (below), the owner of Diamond Foam & Fabric, one of the busiest fabric shops in Los Angeles. He was a wealth of knowledge, and by five o'clock I felt as if I'd taken a crash course. What I learned was that **there are no rules**. You have to **trust your instincts** and buy with your heart. For example, I'd always thought small patterns were for small areas and objects, and big patterns were for large rooms and large pieces of furniture. Jason gave me the confidence to challenge convention.

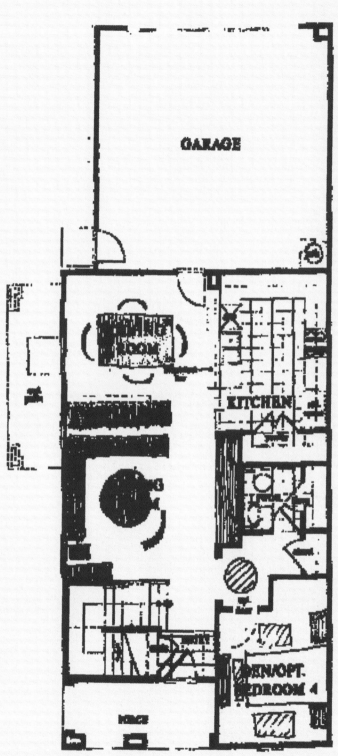

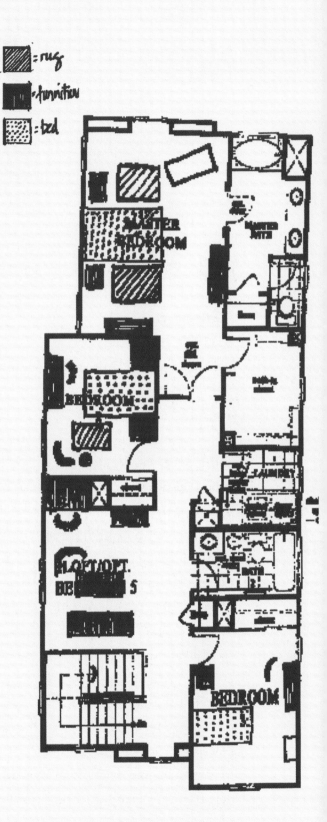

= rug

= furniture

= bed

GARAGE

DINING ROOM

KITCHEN

DEN/OPT. BEDROOM 4

MASTER BEDROOM

MASTER BATH

BEDROOM

LOFT/OPT. BEDROOM 5

LAUNDRY

BEDROOM

FIRST FLOOR

SECOND FLOOR

# Ready, Set, Bid:
# An eBay How-to

DURING THE SIX MONTHS it took to buy everything for the house, I spent many weekends huddled over the computer, oblivious to the outside world. Because the items listed vary so greatly and come from so many disparate places, going on eBay was like visiting infinite numbers of exotic souks and bazaars the world over. One minute, I could have been at an antique shop in the English countryside; the next, a roadside trading post in Santa Fe.

I began the process thinking that because eBay's not hands-on, I wouldn't enjoy it as much as going to a flea market. I was wrong: **eBay has all the thrill of the chase.** You can browse and sift through hundreds of items, even if your browsing is virtual. Because there's so much to see, you get an added perspective. What you thought might be rare may turn out not to be, and vice versa. Unlike flea markets, from which I often come away empty-handed, eBay provides a constant embarrassment of riches. On any given day, there were more than a handful of things I just "had to have," whether I could use them in the eBay house or not.

With so many objects and categories to explore, the hardest part was keeping focused. To help, I drew up furniture plans (opposite) and I wrote up a room-by-room list of what I needed. I carefully tried to estimate size and scale of the furniture I needed. For example, although the wall in the living room could accommodate a ten-foot sofa, I felt that it would have been wrong for the room—too oversized. With eBay, you don't have the luxury of taking things home on approval and returning them if they're not

right. You keep it, give it away, or you can resell it on eBay. I had to be careful. One mistake and I'd blow the budget for an entire room.

The items on my **wish list** ranged from the specific—"two white bar stools for the kitchen"—to the more hazily described (when I wasn't sure what I wanted)—"something to go over the kitchen cabinets—try pots, baskets, vintage metal lunch pails, orange-crate labels." It was equally useful to keep a list of measurements by my computer with the spaces and what I thought the dimensions of major pieces of furniture should be.

I readied myself with a chart for keeping track of objects I bought and what I had to do to transform them—paint them, take them to the framer, the lamp store, the upholsterer, etc.

For those who are new to eBay or are not yet comfortable in traversing its waters, I thought it would be helpful to run through the basics. There are several "how-to" eBay books, including *The Official eBay Bible* by Jim Griffith, that are easy to follow. By and large, though, I relied on friends, who gave me lots of tips that I'll pass along.

## Transformations to make

| Object: | to be done: | where? | date taken |
|---|---|---|---|
| green & white check fabric | a) coffee stain<br>b) made into 2 lampshades | home<br>Carl's | 1/15 |
| white dishtowel red stripes | made into pillows | | 2/3 |
| Hawaiian shirt | framed | Quick frames | 1/20 |
| White pansy coverlet | daybed upholstery | Emilio | 1/10 |
| Oil lamp<br>  clear<br>  white<br>  pewter | to be wired for shades | Carl's | 1/15 |

To begin, go onto the Web and type in *www.ebay.com*; the eBay home page comes up. There you'll find several colorful icons and navigation bars to guide you. Clicking on the word "Buy" in a box at the very top of the page; then clicking on "Learning Center" on the list at the right will provide links to quick on-screen audiovisual tours that walk you through all aspects of eBay.

The first step is to register by clicking on "Register." It's simple and free. It does require creating an eBay user ID and password, which you should jot down somewhere, as you'll need it every time you log on. Registering is useful even if you don't intend to buy anything at first, as it allows you to use a feature called **"My eBay."** This keeps track of items you've looked at as well as, later, those you bid on.

Clicking on "Buy" at the top of the home page takes you to the "Buy" page, which has lists of the general categories you can find on eBay. Typing in some keywords in the "Search" field on the top left brings up a list of items that in some way fit that description. I've found that it often works well to formulate keywords and phrases that correlate to more general design schemes. For example, looking for "Adirondack style" yielded me the hickory chair and log lamps in the guest room.

Wish list

Kitchen:
bar stools
fabric for stool seats & pantry
placemats, napkins
dishes
silverware
glasses or cups & saucers
something to hang on 2 sm
something above cabinet
bowl or cookie jar

No matter what I did, invariably a lot of things came up that didn't relate to what I wanted. That can be frustrating if you have limited time. So you may try to narrow the search by adding or changing the **keywords**. One day, looking for a plantation-style chair, I started by typing in "plantation." The first item that came up was a $3 million plantation in the West Indies! That certainly wasn't on my radar screen as a possible purchase, but it was more fun than another entry that also came up—a remedy for "plantar" warts! I added "chair" and got just what I wanted.

Be careful with using "the," "and," and "or." The search tool on eBay recognizes those words as it would any other terms, not as modifiers. Therefore, you should use them only if you want them to appear in the queried titles. For example, if you search for "peanut butter and jelly," you won't get any searches that don't include all four words. It might be best to just use the more important words, such as "peanut butter jelly." If you put peanut butter in quotes that means you are looking for those words in that order. If you don't use quotes, the words can be in any order.

The minus sign is another good tool for bringing back results that exclude common items that correspond to the same search terms but are totally unrelated to what you want. For example, you could search for "horse" and get 10,000 results; or you could search for "horse -race -carriage -tack" and get only 2,000 results.

If you're looking for something that is generally expensive and don't want to sift through junk, there is a box at the top middle right of the list of items to view that says "Time: ending soonest." Change it by clicking on the pull-down menu so it sorts the results starting with "Price: highest first." You will then be able to look at "fireplace mantles" before the less expensive items such as "mantle clocks" or "firefly pins" come up.

The asterisk is also useful to winnow down what you want. If, for example, you want something like a calendar from 1965, but would be willing to settle for something close, you could enter "196* calendar," and up will come calendars from 1961 to 1969.

Searching for the plural will usually not get you the singular, nor will typing in the singular get you the plural, if the word endings are different.

# Keywords: "Green Ceramic"

# SEARCH TIPS

- Check the box below "keywords" to "search title and description."

- Be careful with your use of "the," "and," and "or." "Lox and bagel" will yield only objects that have all three words.

- If you put keywords in quotes, they come up only in that order.

- The minus sign narrows down your search results. "Black sweater -nylon" would be an example if you're looking for cashmere.

- Entering a word in the singular doesn't yield plurals, and vice versa, if endings are different.

- Once you've found a winning combination, make a note of it or log it into "My eBay" for future use.

- If the object you're looking for tends to be expensive, sort returns by "Price: highest first." That saves you going through junk.

- Keep a list of items and item numbers of objects you like and may wish to pursue in "My eBay."

That means that if you type in "Beanie Babies," you will not get "Beanie Baby," and, if you type in "Beanie Baby," you won't get "Beanie Babies."

More than once, I came up with the perfect search words. A few days later, wanting to pursue a similar item, I couldn't remember what words I'd used in the first place. Formulating the words can be time consuming and, worse, not remembering and having to reconstruct them can make you feel suicidal. Therefore, it's a good idea to put them into **"My Favorite Searches"** in "My eBay." This feature is accessed by going to the "All Favorites" menu on the left, choosing "Searches," and clicking "Add New Search." You can zero in on the search in various ways, including setting a price range and geographical location. Whenever a new listing appears that matches your search term, you will be notified by e-mail.

I learned my lesson when I was pursuing the tiki bar. On one of the first few pages, I found a great one, but I thought I'd scroll through the rest before making a decision. **My instincts were right;** that first one was the best, so I went back but couldn't find it. I spent several hours on two consecutive days searching for it without luck. I thought someone was trying to gaslight me. Finally, on day three, heartsick, I thought I'd try one more time. Eureka! I found it. From that moment on, I've kept a list of what I'm looking for in "My Favorite Searches." You might also note the closing date of the auction. Sellers pay by the day to post their objects; the more they pay, the longer the auction. So, if you're lucky, you'll find an item that will be up for a week or so, giving you time to think about it.

Cruising eBay, looking at different categories, taught me that I was wrong to think eBay would be extremely competitive and that everyone would be after the same objects. Sure, there's a lot of competition on some items. Sometimes, the moniker of people bidding against you is a giveaway as to their level of interest. If I'm bidding on a handkerchief against "Achoo," I know I'm in for a fight.

## Each Room Had Its Own Inspiration Board...

Tiki Loft
Key words: vintage Hawaii tiki.

Collections: vinyl records

Need a tiki Bar

PAINT SCHEDULE   - SHERWIN WILLIAMS

-LOFT
SW7005
PURE WHITE

Wall
mounted
surf board

Have to
have!

Repro
is
OK

MUSCLE
BEACH
PARTY

ALOHA

Staircase
Keywords:
surf board, vintage photos
butterflies
- transition living to loft

Gidget

PAINT SCHEDULE   - SHERWIN WILLIAMS

-STAIRCASE
SW6478
WATERY

HAWAII
BY CLIPPER
PAN AMERICAN WORLD AIRWAYS

eBay is different from most other auctions in that a vast number of items are available at any given time. The speed at which items come and go is also a major factor. If you don't find what you're looking for one day, come back the next, and you may find twelve new listings, all filling the bill.

Once you pick an item and click on the listing, you come to a page with a picture and a description, current bid price, number of bids, seller's e-mail address (and feedback rating), current high bidder's e-mail address, amount of time left in the auction, and shipping and insurance information. This window also contains the box where you can place your bid. Many buyers who don't have the time to frequently check leave a maximum bid. eBay will automatically up your bid by one increment anytime someone else bids against you until you win or the bidding reaches your maximum. If you're outbid, you get an e-mail. Some objects being sold have a "Buy It Now" feature, which allows you to bypass the auction process and pay the seller a prescribed amount he lists. Either way, what you buy or bid on is automatically recorded in "My eBay" and is easily retrieved.

There are other buyer features accessible in "Tools," found by clicking on "Services" at the very top of the home page, and then clicking on "Buying Recources page." One of these is wireless phone notification. A friend told me that one day when he was in college, he left an exam, turned on his cell, and learned via a text message that he'd been outbid. With only a few minutes left in the auction, he didn't have time to make it all the way home. He ran to a friend's dorm on campus, only to find her second-floor room locked. He jumped on the air conditioner, hoisted himself up to her balcony, and entered her room through the sliding glass doors. He got on in time but was outbid. All for a Dolly Parton lamp. Recently, when I spoke to the same friend, he told me excitedly that he'd just bought a pair of seventh-row seats to a Dolly Parton concert—on eBay, of course.

As with the Dolly Parton lamp, don't be lulled into thinking that no one else is bidding and that you don't have to bid your max. You may be going along, sure you're going to get the object, and then someone else uses a sniper program, such as AuctionSniper or AuctionBlitz. That means that a few seconds before the end of the auction, a sniper may execute a bid higher than yours by an increment, and you lose.

Take your time and figure out **how much the object is really worth to you.** If you "have to have" it, add on another 10 or 20 percent to the most you want to bid. I call it the "love factor." If a green Weller pot is worth approximately $150 and you have to pay $180 to get it, don't worry. Five years from now, you'll still adore it and won't remember that you paid more than you wanted. Besides, with market changes, the vase may be worth twice what you paid.

An e-mail will notify you that you've won an item. The seller will tell you which **payment methods** are acceptable to him. Although some sellers are willing to take checks or money orders, most sellers and buyers these days prefer PayPal, a third-party payment system owned by eBay. Once you register, PayPal lets you pay by credit card or draws the funds from a bank account you've designated.

On several occasions, both during an auction and after I've lost one, I've gotten e-mail from someone who has a similar object for sale. I wonder if some sellers do this so they don't have to pay eBay's commissions. I'm a little wary of these situations, especially if the seller asks you to send the money in an unsecured way or if he's only willing to take a money order. I usually ask them to list the object on eBay and go through the system.

I made so many purchases for the house that I created **templates** (pages 208–9) **that I send to sellers**. One confirms the sale and asks the seller for his payment preferences. It also allows you to provide the seller with your name and address so he can calculate shipping costs. The second is a confirmation to send with your payment.

One of the most important things I learned is that you have to **keep a careful eye on the shipping costs**. Some sellers charge more than they should as a way of making extra money. I didn't realize this until I was well into the process, when I bought a chair from a man who lived about an hour from me. He told me that shipping the chair would cost $170. That seemed exorbitant, so I asked for his address and told him I'd drive over and pick it up instead. Suddenly, he found a new shipper—for a fraction of the cost. From then on, before I left a bid, I asked for the approximate shipping costs and negotiated accordingly. Most of the major carriers, from UPS to the U.S. Postal Service, have rate calculators on their websites, and you can check prices yourself.

In each transaction, the seller and buyer have the opportunity to score each other by leaving feedback—positive, negative, or neutral. Look at the seller's feedback score, located on the right side of the page. It represents the number of positive ratings minus the negatives that buyers have left. If the seller has a good track record, you can rest easier that the transaction will go smoothly, your new acquisition will be as described, and it will arrive in one piece. If a seller has no feedback or very little, be wary. Of course, we've all heard horror stories about sellers who falsify good ratings and steal identities in order to reel in unsuspecting buyers. That happens more frequently in the area of electronics, where a digital camera is sold every ninety

dining room

Plates on walls

Shiny white table

Ironstone

WIN WILLIAMS

dining
dining wall

accent colors
on stencilled wall

Dining Area
Key words:
    Cottage, garden

Collections:
    majolica
    Ironstone

to look for:
    green + wh. fabric
    old table
    chairs
    green glasses
    old silverware
    candle holders

different indoor
Chairs outdoor

Fresh Flowers

+door

This fine fabric is from
The Silk Trading Co.™

bar

seconds. The sheer volume portends problems. By contrast, with household goods and collectibles, the rate of problems is only a tiny percentage. Nonetheless, with the endless ways a scammer can take your money and run, you have to be careful.

Without being able to see the actual object, I find it hard to have the confidence to make expensive purchases. Sometimes, for a break from the eBay house, I'd look at the bidding on Hermès handbags. They can easily go for thousands. I've written an article on them, and I've looked at a lot of them over the years, but could anyone see enough details in a thumbnail photo to tell real from fake? (I'm not sure I can tell the difference in person.) Sometimes, if there's major money at stake, eBay bidding is not for the faint of heart.

As there's always a risk that the piece you're bidding on will arrive and isn't or doesn't look like what you bid on, I made a decision that I wasn't going to drive myself crazy if any purchase under $25 didn't work out. After all, Christmas was coming, and I could always give it away. Whenever I bid into the hundreds, however, that was another story. If it isn't as the seller described, I would contact eBay; if the fault was mine, I would try to give it away or resell it on eBay or Craig's List.

**Browsing on eBay is so much fun** that it's an end in itself—like shopping. I love to shop and don't feel obliged to buy anything. My husband is the opposite. He wants to buy what he needs and get out of the store as swiftly as possible. The same is true on eBay. Bert's in and out in a few minutes. By contrast, I can be amused just seeing what's available and what others are bidding on, especially outrageous objects. Aimless browsing on eBay has, for many, replaced late night TV. I remember when I was growing up, after we kids and Dad went to bed, Mother would sit up and watch Johnny Carson. That was her private time. She'd knit, write letters, and simply unwind. Today, going online, particularly eBay, provides the same relaxing experience—a good way to come down off a long hard day. Sometimes I browse; other times I'm on a mission. Still other times, I'm mesmerized and buy something I don't need. Worse, I buy it and pay more than I should.

There are times I think I'm addicted. To me, going into eBay is like putting on the red shoes and being unable to stop dancing. One night when my husband was away on business, I went on an eBay bender. I bid for six different plates, and, not sure I was going to win the auctions, I bid on another six. In the end, I got ten, and my table has room for only four. The next day, I decided to hang up my red shoes and swear off eBay for a while. That lasted for about two days until I realized that I had to have two small pieces of needlepoint. "They're all I need to finish off our living room," I told myself. Famous last words.

Crazes come and go, and you have to be careful not to get carried away. For a while, college kids were selling their used underwear on eBay (shown on the usually hot-bodied males or females). They'd regularly go for $7 to $10. It was a joke, but used underwear is no longer sold. (Of course, neither are child porn, weapons, drugs, and pirated or counterfeit DVDs and CDs.) Beanie Babies were another craze. They used to be the number one eBay seller. A rare Beanie Baby, at one point, would have brought as much as $3,000 to $5,000. Now a great one goes for about $150. Thank heavens I missed the Beanie Baby bubble.

**All in all, eBay is a trip; it's practical, relaxing, invigorating, and it's a whole lot of fun!**

# The Sellers

SURE, EBAY'S ABOUT COMMERCE. There are twelve million listings a day. Major companies like Sears and Motorola sell goods on eBay. Antique shops, flea marketeers, and secondhand dealers are sellers. Many brick-and-mortar operations have closed and are exclusively selling on eBay. Others, who are keeping their facilities, view eBay as an additional venue. Astoundingly, more than 400,000 individuals make their living by selling on eBay. (One seller told me she turned her two extra bedrooms into a packing and shipping assembly line.)

But eBay's not all about commerce. It's an enormous cultural phenomenon—a national pastime, a lifestyle. eBay satisfies the need to **reach out and communicate.** There's a lot of schmoozing in it. Sellers and other bidders want to know why you bought something and where and how you're going to use it. They get up close and personal very quickly. Recently, my friend's mother, an avid collector of salt and pepper shakers, had a cancer operation. My friend spent a good part of her day away from the hospital answering inquiries from vendors and collectors all over the world whom her mother had "met" via eBay. Many were genuinely concerned, and some even sent flowers and cards (electronic, of course!).

The chatting goes on throughout the process. Once, I was bidding on a small table by the Finnish designer Eero Saarinen. After some back-and-forth e-mails, the seller couldn't wait to tell me a "small world" story. "Oddly enough, I just brought home a neat old wooden prune shipping box that I found recently at a garage sale. I noticed that ink stamped on the ends of the box was the label for the Pansy Brand California Santa Clara Prunes. The prunes were packed by Guggenheim & Company. I guess prune packing and Guggenheims go together."

Of the over 400 objects I bought, one stood out—a hanky. The hanky cost only a few dollars, yet the seller spent a good deal of time carefully and lovingly placing it in tissue, wrapping it as a present, and even finishing it off with a bow and a card. It's so special, I still haven't had the heart to unwrap it (opposite). To me, this package says it all about eBay sellers.

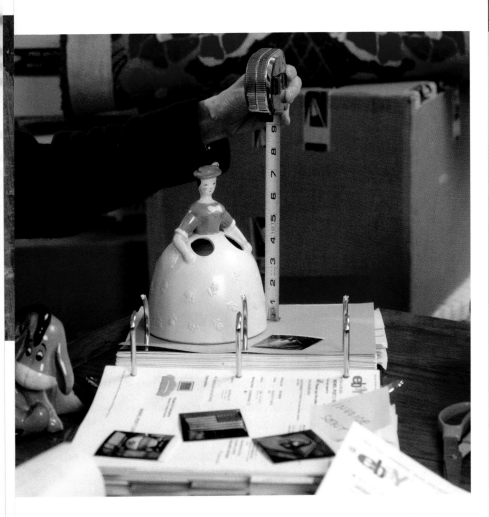

sold me the aloha shirt for the same room. I'm not sure whether his name refers to his packing abilities or his sexual preference.

Recently, there was a documentary about a man who sold everything he owned on eBay. He drove all over the country and met the hundreds of people who'd bought his stuff. My eBay project is almost the complete opposite. I've collected valuable pieces of other people's lives from all over the world and assembled them together in one place. A dining room table and chairs, for example, come from four different states, a watering can from France, ironstone from England. That we can participate in an international market with such ease is endlessly astonishing and changes all of our lives.

# eBay Tips

I can't imagine why there isn't an eBay Anonymous. If there was one, I'd be a charter member. If I see something in a store, or if a friend has something I admire, I run home and get on eBay to see if I can find one like it, cheaper. If I go on eBay after dinner, the next thing I know, it's 2:00 a.m.

Opposite are some guidelines I've devised for decorating your home on eBay. I hope they'll be helpful.

1. Think before you buy. Don't plunge in and start buying without a game plan. Take your time to glean inspiration from shelter magazines, stylebooks, friends' homes, and shops. Don't be afraid to borrow other people's good ideas.

2. Get organized and stay organized. Consider the space and what you're trying to accomplish. Start an inspiration board. That way, you can tack up photos, color chips, fabric samples, and all the lists you may need.

3. Have patience. Don't worry if your dream object doesn't come along the first day. It may take a while. You may need to modify your search by changing the words you've typed in to describe what you want. If you're looking for a rattan chair, for example, you might try "bamboo" or "reed."

4. Check the seller's feedback, especially if the object you're buying is expensive. Try to get the seller's name, address, and phone number. Whatever you do, don't give him your Social Security number or any information not relevant to shipping. Don't be afraid to ask questions, and if you're uncomfortable with the answers, don't bid. To find out if the seller is knowledgeable in a particular area, ask what similar items he's sold.

5. Familiarize yourself with the features of online auctions and use them—such as "My eBay," which lists what you're bidding on and what you've bought.

6. If you have to have something, add another 10 to 20 percent to the maximum you're willing to bid. I call it "the love factor." There's nothing worse than losing the object you desperately want. Two years from now, you won't remember that you paid more than you'd wanted.

7. Sometimes you have to fix what you buy. It could be as little as using some glue. Consider what transformations must be made and what costs will be incurred. Repairing, altering, and improving things can be easy and a lot of fun.

8. Keep a list of all the things that might interest you, and their lot numbers, in "Save Search" and use it. It's too hard to remember the keywords you've used.

9. A seller's moniker can tell you how serious he is. If "Fiesta Frank" is selling Fiestaware, he probably knows what he's doing.

10. Don't be afraid of making a mistake. You can always resell what you don't like on eBay!

# The Arrival: Here It Comes!

THERE'S NOTHING MORE EXCITING than the moment when an eBay package arrives. From my home office, I see the UPS truck coming up the street. The driver rings the bell: I run to the door. He's even more attractive than the UPS guy in *Legally Blonde*, and we're on a first-name basis. If he weren't married, I'd have all my single friends shipping UPS and learning the film's "bend-and-snap" method to attract him.

After a flurry of buying, I can receive as many as a dozen packages a day. My friend Dan's letter carrier, Cynthia, took early retirement because of all the eBay packages Dan received.

## My garage and living room were filled to the brim...

This morning, there are only two packages. I pick one up and jiggle it; it tinkles. Uh-oh. Broken glass. I put that aside and pick up the other. As I cut the tape, pieces of Russian newspapers fall out. I extrapolate that the seller is a Russian smoker (the paper smelled like snuffed-out cigarettes. Ugh!). I'm jittery. "Would the vase I bought look like it did in the photo? Is it really as described?" I'm crazy to be nervous; most of the objects I bought cost less than $50. Not to worry in this case; the vase looks great, and I'm thrilled.

**LEFT:**
This brand new elm (with a dark mahogany stain) cane chair arrived in perfect condition. It was one of my early finds, and I was delighted with the results. If only the rest had gone as smoothly!

**OPPOSITE:**
Forget entertaining! My living room was turned into a warehouse for the eBay project.

I thought that my own living room and garage would be big enough to store everything I bought while the eBay house was being built, but they weren't. Therefore I had to take space in a local warehouse to store the overflow.

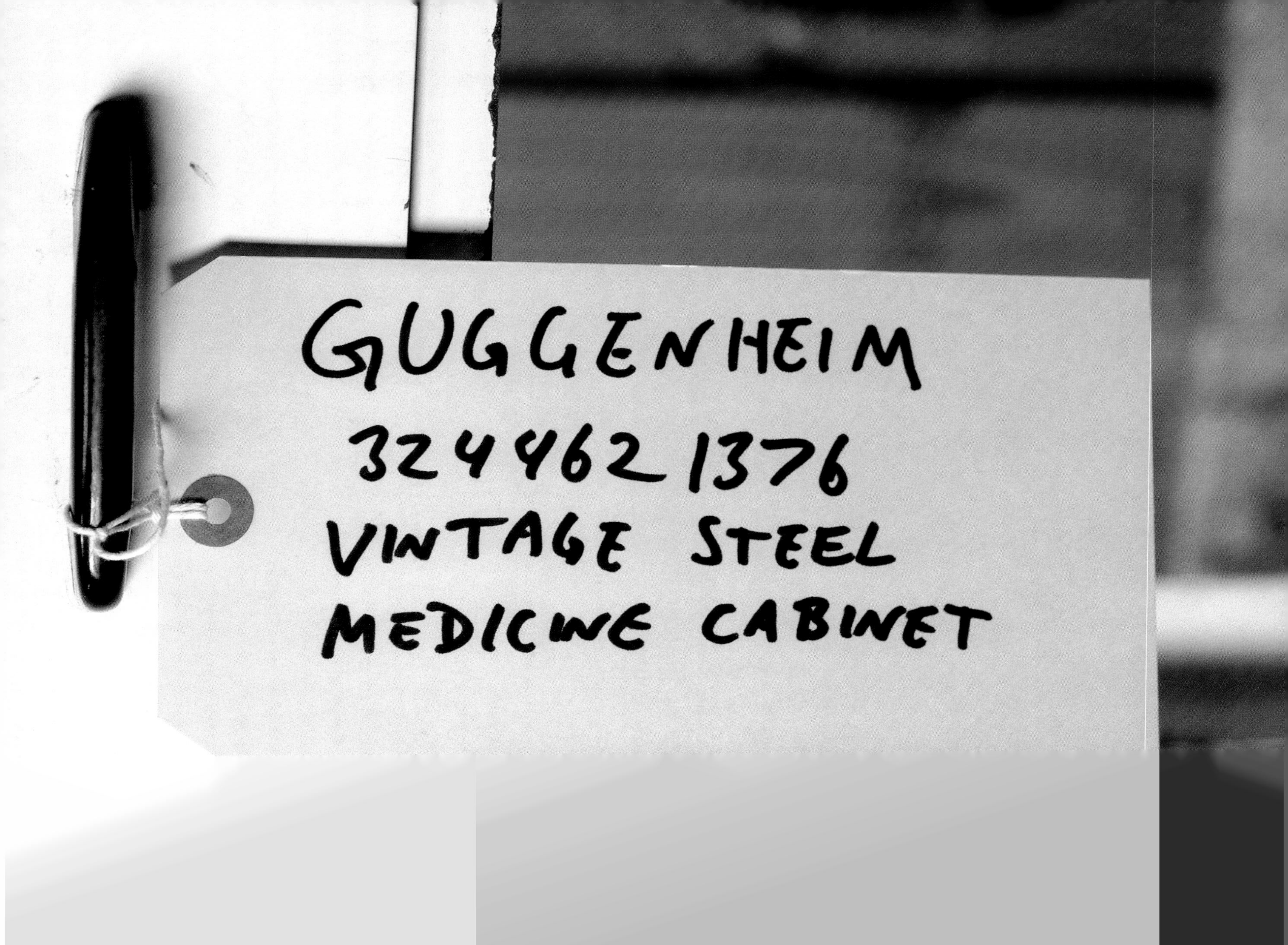

GUGGENHEIM
324 462 1376
VINTAGE STEEL
MEDICINE CABINET

# Moving In

MOVING IN WAS A BREEZE, maybe because I'd marked all the boxes. The benefit of good planning and organization paid off.

Most people who use eBay to decorate buy a few decorative objects, or at most do a room. If you're planning to buy a houseful of objects, and move in all at once, as I did, you really have to be organized. I had no idea that it takes so many objects to fill a house (I bought over 400), and you have to be careful that the little ones don't get lost in the shuffle. I'd stored the biggest objects in a warehouse and the smaller things at my home, so a truck made two stops en route to the eBay house. I packed the small breakables, like vases, in bubblewrap and boxes and took them to the house in my car.

## TIPS FOR MOVING IN

- Save boxes from the bigger items that you bought on eBay or get some throwaways from a supermarket.

- Have plenty of newspaper, bubble wrap, tape, labels, and "Fragile" stickers on hand.

- Make a list of rooms and number them. Label boxes (on all sides) and anything you wrap by room number.

# II. THE ROOMS

**WHAT I DID** in the eBay house isn't as much about decorating as it is about simply putting together a lot of ideas and objects that appealed to me and I hoped might appeal to others. My goal was to create the kind of relaxed, interesting but comfortable home that most of us associate with great wealth—for a lot less money. For each member of my imagined family of four—a husband, wife, twelve-year-old daughter, and nine-year-old son—I made up likes, dislikes, interests, favorite colors, and so forth, which helped me create rooms with character.

59

# The Entrance

Total Cost: $578.73

DO YOU STRUGGLE every time you come home to find a place to set down your mail, shopping bags, keys, wallet, hat, and coat? Do you long for a staging area, somewhere to put all the things you want to take with you the next day? It would need to be attractive as well as functional, as it's the first thing you see when you enter the house. The "Shaker-style coat rack/portmanteau," NIB (new in box), was perfect and set the tone for the rest of the house. Its faux-distressed finish (painted to look like it had wear) was a pleasant surprise, as it didn't show on the thumbnail photo the seller submitted to eBay.

To complement its clean lines, I bought an Early American firkin (used to carry salt or sugar) and a repro of a flag. You can never go wrong using a flag or an image of one. A pastel rag rug provided another countrylike element. The Stetson wasn't my first choice; I'd bought a Burberry scarf, but I couldn't resist keeping that for myself.

Drawing ideas from the classic American porch, I chose items that were friendly and familiar and that went with the arts-and-crafts façade.

## Costs: ENTRANCE

| | | |
|---|---|---|
| 1. | Portmanteau (Coat Rack Storage Bench) | $196.98 |
| 2. | Old Gray Firkin (Sugar Bucket) | $92.00 |
| 3. | Old Sage Green Round Splint Basket | $49.00 |
| 4. | Stetson Hat | $35.00 |
| 5. | Print of Colonial American Flag | $34.02 |
| 6. | Antique Multicolored Rag Rug | $24.99 |
| | SUBTOTAL | $431.99 |
| | SHIPPING | $81.79 |
| | TRANSFORMATION (framing) | $64.95 |
| | TOTAL | $578.73 |

# The Living Room

**Total Cost:** $9,973.70

MOST FORMAL LIVING ROOMS are wasted space: They're stiff and uncomfortable. So why not make your living room a weekend fantasy? With a country cottage in mind, I aimed for the feel of a relaxed, summer getaway, the kind of room in which you don't have to worry if the dog jumps on the sofa. Cottage design is all about details, so I installed white moldings and box shutters (KB Home paid), which contrasted beautifully with the walls painted the color of key lime pie. Instead of putting a TV unit in the alcove, I asked KB Home to build in a bench (page 76) and overhead shelf. These elements added charm to the room even before I started decorating it.

My first buy was a sectional sofa (#4). It anchors the space, adds to the room's coziness, and separates the living and dining areas. It was the most expensive purchase for the house ($1,999). Not only was it new, straight from the factory, but I was amazed to learn from the vendor that I could choose the upholstery fabric. I selected white denim—just what I wanted. It was my first major purchase, and I held my breath. The die was cast.

| | | |
|---|---|---|
| 1. | Mission Rocking Chair c. 1910 | $510.00 |
| 2. | Adirondack Chair | $120.00 |
| 3. | Coffee Table w/ Pedestal Base (and Ladder-back Chairs) | $460.00 |
| 4. | Sectional Sofa | $1,999.00 |
| 5. | White Sofa Side Table w/Roses Decals | $29.99 |
| 6. | White Wicker Magazine Table | $81.02 |
| 7. | White Aladdin Oil Lamps (2) | $175.00 |
| 8. | Clear Glass Aladdin Oil Lamp | $35.00 |
| 9. | Stained Glass Window | $95.00 |
| 10. | Pierced Rectangular Architectural Wall Element | $17.99 |
| 11. | Oil Painting of Pansies | $685.20 |
| 12. | Wooden Architectural Corbels | $26.99 |
| 13. | Green Arts and Crafts Pottery (16 pieces) | $1,435.29 |
| 14. | Dried Hydrangeas | $34.00 |
| 15. | Birdhouse | $11.35 |
| 16. | Cast-Iron Sundial | $24.00 |
| 17. | Floral Tea Pot Set | $86.00 |
| 18. | Hurricane Candle Shades | $99.98 |
| 19. | Vases for Flowers | $40.76 |
| 20. | Books and Magazines | $16.99 |
| 21. | Seagrass Rug | $99.00 |
| 22. | Pillows (already made) | $64.00 |
| 23. | Fabrics for Pillows & Cushions in Niche and on Sofa | $381.67 |
| 24. | Seashells | $76.98 |
| 25. | Ironstone Pitcher | $24.99 |
| | Long White Sofaback Table | $300.00 |
| | Green Rattan Table | $324.99 |
| | Round Wall Mirror with Pierced Decorative Border | $14.99 |
| | Silver Finish Wall Mirror | $54.99 |
| | Set of 4 Gilt Mirrors | $14.99 |
| | Model Sailboat | $79.00 |
| | Hooked Rugs | $118.64 |

| | |
|---|---|
| SUBTOTAL | $7,537.80 |
| SHIPPING | $1,612.25 |
| TRANSFORMATIONS (cutting and painting table, pillows and upholstery, lampshades and wiring, framing) | $823.65 |
| TOTAL | $9,973.70 |

# FABRICS FOR PILLOWS

When I was a teenager, I won a regional sewing contest with a print shirtwaist dress. Could I even match seams now? Could I make piping?

In the end I was short on time and realized that the dozen or more pillows I wanted would have taken days to make. So I took the fabric to a shop specializing in pillows. Each pillow (welding the seams, insetting a zipper, and stuffing) cost $38 on average. (I'm sure I could have gotten a better price if I comparative shopped or negotiated up front for the group.) I particularly loved putting one fabric on the front of a pillow (a print) and another on the back (a stripe).

**the alcove** I've always loved window seats. To me they're romantic. So I took the alcove, designed as a media center, and converted it to a window seat. Never mind that there's no window. Here's where I used the Ralph Lauren stripe-and-flower fabric. (Don't worry, Mom, it worked out. I used a different fabric for the sides and bottom.) It cost $155 to have the seat cushion made. All but one of the pillows were done inexpensively using vintage dish towels and remnants. A ready-made pillow with a red geranium pattern was probably made by cutting up a vintage tablecloth. What a great thing to do with old stained tablecloths: You can cut them up and make pillows from the good parts.

# BRINGING THE INTERIOR TO LIFE WITH FABRICS

A little fabric goes a long way. Old bedspreads, remnants, and odds and ends were easily transformed into upholstery, seat cushions, drapes, pillows, and placemats.

**antiquing fabrics** An easy way to give new fabric character is by making it look old. The traditional method for antiquing fabric is by tea staining. The truth is, soaking fabric in coffee is faster and easier. I simply dumped a jar of coffee into a big vat of water (it doesn't have to be warm) and mixed it (opposite). Fabric takes only a minute or so to start darkening. Not wanting to change the color too drastically, I pulled it out after just a few minutes. After you take the fabric out of the coffee, be sure to rinse it immediately or the darkening action will continue. Then wring it, and put it over a line or lay it out flat to dry.

# PAINTING THE HOUSE:
# COLOR MAKES A DIFFERENCE

The conventional wisdom is that if your house has "good bones," whatever you put in it will look great. I guess that's true. If you have an old home with high ceilings, fireplaces, bay windows, or paneled walls, it's hard to go wrong. But if your house is new, like this one, and doesn't have a lot of old architectural details, what can you do to give it character? Painting the walls can be a relatively inexpensive, quick fix. It's like coloring your hair; you can be a redhead one minute and blonde the next, and it doesn't have to be a forever commitment. Be adventurous. If you don't like the color, you can always paint it again.

The only walls painted white (Sherwin Williams) were in the kitchen, the kids' bathroom (to give a clean, crisp look), and the loft, as a backdrop for the busy vinyl records and loud Hawaiian prints. For the other rooms, I chose different colors and techniques to fit the mood I was trying to achieve. KB Home took care of the solid-colored walls, and I supplied the paint for all the patterned walls.

**living room/stairwell** The walls in the living room were painted different colors—the stair wall blue and the rest of the living room green—to delineate a change in the use of space. Frankly, the green turned out closer to mint green than I would have liked. I'd made my decision from a small color card in the paint store, which was a mistake. I should have bought a small can and painted a large swatch on the wall before painting the whole room. Next time.

# TURNING A DINING TABLE INTO A COFFEE TABLE

Not everything I bought was perfect and ready to go. Many things needed assembling, painting, sewing, repair, or other transformations. Part of the fun was envisioning an object's possibilities and doing the hands-on work required. When I couldn't do something myself, like framing, upholstery, or wiring lamps, I took the object to a professional.

Finding the right coffee table was next to impossible, so I bought a round pedestal dining table and cut it down. I think that the height of a coffee table should be the height of the seat of a chair or sofa—anywhere from twelve to eighteen inches. Dining tables are about twenty-nine inches, so I had to cut off around eleven inches or more. This wasn't as hard as it looked. Victorian tables often have flourishes on their pedestals, and I made the cut next to a ring where the seam would be less noticeable (top). I lightly coated both sides with carpenter's glue and then used screws to keep the table in place. No clamping was necessary (center). I painted the table white (bottom) and later added a green trim. It came with chairs, which I also painted white. They looked terrific in the dining area.

## details:

A little wicker goes a long way in creating an indoor/outdoor feel to the room.

**details:**
The tea set may look like a meaningless prop, but it's not. It's there to remind us to slow down and enjoy life.

# ARTS AND CRAFTS POTTERY

The Industrial Revolution produced a lot of boring and unattractive household objects, along with poor working conditions. Reformers argued that handmade products would work better and enhance society on functional and aesthetic levels. Pottery makers in the early years of the twentieth century responded to this call by creating tiles, lamp bases, bowls, and vases that were not only functional, but beautiful as well. Why were so many green? Because the movement urged artists to use material and colors that approximated nature.

Glazes, factory of origin, artist, and size are all factors in determining a piece's rarity and price, and if you're not an expert, it's hard to navigate the waters. Connoisseurship is difficult enough in person, and as I mentioned, I don't know how collectors make decisions looking at eBay's thumbnail photos. I bought a few pieces bearing familiar names (like Grueby, Jemerick, and Ephraim), and then, feeling uncomfortable about buying blindly and not wanting to overspend, I turned to bidding on cheaper examples. Only one was a real dud. So what! I put it on the high shelf in the alcove where no one could examine it closely. After all, it's the look that counts.

1.

2.

4.

5.

# TIPS FOR BUYING ARTS AND CRAFTS POTTERY

- Ask the vendor if the colors in the photo are true. Ask questions about the glaze, chips, etc.

- Ask how he knows it's by so and so, and ask to see a photo of the signature.

- Check other sales of similar objects either on eBay or in price guides available.

## Costs: ARTS AND CRAFTS GREEN POTTERY

| | | |
|---|---|---|
| 1. | Jemerick Vase - bulbous shape with leaf pattern | $49.99 |
| 2. | Arts and Crafts Poppy Vase with repeating poppy buds | $112.00 |
| 3. | Gingko Vase | $68.00 |
| 4. | Tall Matte Vase with long neck | $82.01 |
| 5. | Ephraim Pine Cone Vase with 3 sets of pine cones cascading | $155.00 |
| 6. | Roseville Matte Green Vase with two handles and long neck | $272.00 |
| | Grueby Oval-shaped Planter | $19.99 |
| | Jemerick Vase - bulbous shape | $49.99 |
| | Arts and Crafts Mission Vase | $63.75 |
| | Van Briggle Bud Vase - engraved on four sides | $66.55 |
| | Van Briggle Bud Vase - water lily on one side | $66.55 |
| | Van Briggle Pottery Seashell | $71.00 |
| | Low, Wide ZSC Zanesville Dish | $71.96 |
| | Zanesville Matte Vase | $75.00 |
| | Hampshire Arts and Crafts Vase - small globe with drip-style glaze | $157.50 |
| | Jemerick Pottery Vase - taller, narrower shape with leaf pattern | $54.00 |
| | TOTAL | $1,435.29 |

3.

6.

## details:

I placed some of the pots on a sofa side table, one of many objects I bought for the house that far surpassed my expectations. I couldn't tell from the small photo that the table had been painted by hand and that there were cut-out pieces of paper printed in a floral pattern (wallpaper?) decoupaged on the shelves. The distressed finish and a slightly yellowish varnish gave the table its shabby chic charm.

# A VISIT TO A LAMP STORE

Some of the lamps arrived with faulty wiring, so I took them to Carl's Custom Lamps & Shades (opposite). While I was there, I became fascinated by the brightly colored shades Carl had on display and decided to order all the shades I needed there. I might have been able to buy some on eBay, but it would have been too time consuming. This way was probably more cost/time effective and I got exactly what I wanted. Some were ready-made, like the white ones in the master suite (right top), but others were made to order. The pair of shades for the log lamps in the guest room (right bottom) were made with two

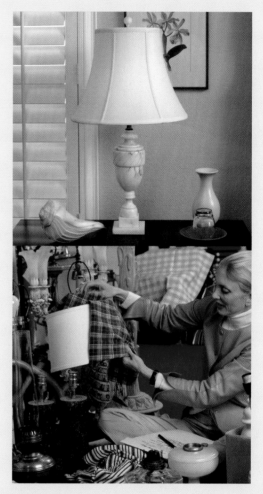

different fabrics I bought on eBay, one a plaid (to trim), the other, striped (left). I couldn't believe how much a shade can enhance a room!

## oil lamps

There's something romantic about the flickering light of an oil lamp. Today, there's even a club of devotees who collect them, and old Aladdin lamps are especially prized. I bought several for the house and electrified them. Don't tell the club, please! I put them in the living room—two white opalescent lamps are on the table behind the sofa (right) and a clear glass one is on a sofa side table—and the bedroom—a pewter one that cost $79.99 (left). The green-and-white-checked cotton, coffee-stained to look old (see page 68), was used to make the lampshades for the pair (right).

# DINING AREA WALL: HOW TO STENCIL

The back wall in the dining area is key. It's the first thing you see when you enter the house. I thought a stenciled pattern would break up the big, flat expanse and provide some texture. I took a three-hour lesson from Doug Funkhouser (above), a professional faux painter and fabric designer, and convinced him to lend me a stencil he'd already cut. Hiring a pro to teach me the technique cost a lot less than the thousands of dollars I would have had to pay painters to do it for me. I was surprised at how easy it was to do a passable job and what fun.

## stenciling

**CUTTING** (top left and right) Doug Funkhouser showing me how to cut a stencil.

**PAINTING** (center) Brushing the paint through the stencil.

**BLENDING** (right) The secret is to put only a small amount of paint on a rag at a time.

**POSITIONING** (opposite) Brushing the paint through the stencil to create a repeat pattern.

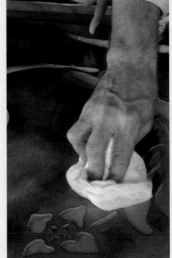

I started with the green wall already dry. (KB Home had painted the wall green.) The darker green was a Sears indoor paint I bought locally called Avocado Heather Medium Deep #EE213. The blue was also a Sears paint, Oceanic #GG341. Each color was mixed 50:50 with a Sears opaque glaze. The secret is to put only a little paint on a rag at a time, not to douse it, and to pat lightly. Am I ready to faux paint Versailles? Not just yet.

DINING AREA CHAIRS

Finding a set of dining room chairs
I liked and could afford proved impossible.
I had to think out of the box. It was easier
and cheaper to buy sets of twos or threes.
I tried for "ice cream parlor chairs" and
bentwood, curved-back cafe chairs, called
"Thonet" after the maker. Ladder-back
chairs had come with the table I'd cut
down for the living room, so I used them
as well. I painted all of them white and
used the same fabric for the seat cushions.
Somehow, it worked.

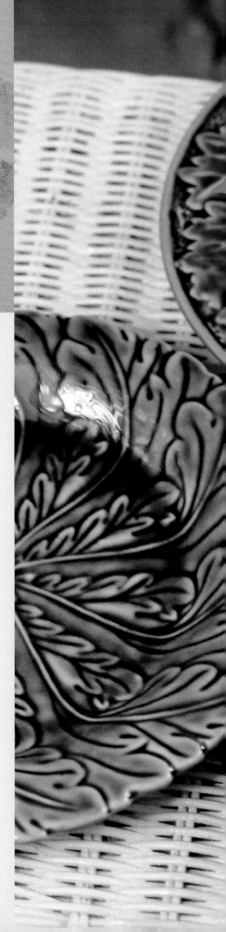

## Ironstone

It's interesting to think that ironstone, which is so widely collected and adored, started life as a simple, functional dishware for the masses. It was the Tupperware of the nineteenth century. Invented in England, it was exported to American farms as a durable, inexpensive way to feed itinerant harvest workers. To relieve its plainness, manufacturers added rural American motifs such as wheat or corn, which were calculated to appeal to the consumer. Ironstone's still appealing, but it's outgrown its homespun connotation. Today, it's prized and pricey. On eBay, however, you can still find remarkable bargains.

## Majolica

Walking through antique shows, I'm always drawn to stands specializing in majolica. I love the bright colors and textures. The term "majolica" derives from a nineteenth-century trade name of a type of pottery produced in France and Holland based on the word *maiolica* (late Renaissance earthenware, fired at a very low temperature). Today, it's used for any high-relief plates, particularly green ones with leaf patterns. Sure, it would be great to collect antique Minton majolica at $1,000 a plate, but who can afford it?

I used a vintage 1950s dogwood tablecloth and napkins on the dining table, just like the one my mother used for her canasta parties. I laughed as I was bidding on it, wondering if it was the very one my mother had—or if it would make me a better canasta player.

# The Kitchen

**Total Cost: $886.88**

TWO GOOD THINGS about an all-white kitchen: It's easy to keep clean, and it forms a terrific backdrop for colorful kitchen collectibles. I could have gone crazy buying vintage cookie jars, mixing bowls, and the like, and had to hold myself back.

I had no luck finding a large blackboard, but hanging the two smaller ones, one over the other (right), worked well. Opposite, on the back wall, I put up three rug beaters, chosen for their playful silhouettes. They were made of metal wire shaped into delightful images, such as a house and a gingerbread man. They're so simple that they look like the most precious Early American folk art masterpieces. And the best part? They cost only a few dollars apiece.

## the unexpected: rug beaters

To stay within budget, I struggled to stick to my lists and not be seduced by things I didn't need. Nonetheless, there were some terrific objects I couldn't resist, including things I never knew existed. For example, while searching for "rugs" on eBay, images of "rug beaters" kept popping up. I'd only vaguely known what a rug beater was before I started this process and never knew they came in such whimsical shapes.

## Costs: KITCHEN

| | | |
|---|---|--:|
| 1. | Bar Stools (2) | $116.00 |
| 2. | Bauer Pottery Mixing Bowl | $21.60 |
| 3. | McCoy Yelloware Bowl | $99.99 |
| 4. | Orange Juice Set by Hocking | $6.99 |
| 5. | Persimmon Fiestaware 5 pc setting | $17.50 |
| 6. | Sunflower Fiestaware 5 pc setting | $16.95 |
| 7. | Red-handled Stainless Flatware Set (St/8) | $36.50 |
| 8. | Curtain Fragment for Placemats | $18.50 |
| 9. | Vintage Blackboard/Abacus | $36.50 |
| 10. | Vintage Blackboard/Abacus with painted designs | $22.28 |
| 11. | Orange Crate Labels (11) | $68.00 |
| | Rug Beaters | $32.51 |
| | SUBTOTAL | $493.32 |
| | SHIPPING | $74.19 |
| | TRANSFORMATIONS (upholstery and framing) | $319.37 |
| | TOTAL | $886.88 |

# Fiestaware

Fiestaware, with its bold forms and bright colors, originated as everyday china in the mid-1930s. Collectors today look for rarity of color and shape and, of course, condition. A serious collector would turn up his nose at my buying contemporary reissues, but I don't care. They look the same, and they're a lot cheaper. Dishtowels, or a curtain fragment, like this one, cut in half, make perfect placemats.

## inspiration fabric for chair cushions

To go with the Fiestaware, I envisioned a bright vegetable-print fabric for the bar-stool cushions and pantry door. I saw a lively print of red and yellow hot peppers at a fabric store. I thought, "If only I could find a print half this good on eBay, I'd be thrilled." Surprisingly, I found one I liked a lot better. Less dense, it depicted a variety of colorful vegetables (opposite). There were eleven yards, more than enough to do what I wanted, at only $60.69 (that came to $5.52 a yard). The seller emphasized that the fabric was "in excellent condition and without odor!" The "without odor" part was comforting. I don't mind the smell of mothballs, or someone else's perfume, but there's nothing worse than opening a package and getting a whiff of stale cigarettes. There should be a check box on the eBay search page: "Comes from a smoke-free home."

## an ebay find...

There were times when what I found on eBay was
better than what I found in stores.

## orange crate labels

A foot-high space above the kitchen cabinets—twenty-two running feet, to be exact—was crying out for a collection of something. Baskets, pottery, even metal lunch pails came to mind. But orange crate labels were perfect. Not only were they the right size, but they

also gave a nostalgic nod to the location of the model home (Valencia, California), once one of the orange-growing capitals of America.

In the late nineteenth century, orange sellers tried to make their brands more recognizable by gluing colorful labels to the wooden shipping boxes. By the 1920s and '30s, over 2,000 companies were producing these labels. The lettering was done by one set of artists, and the scenes were done by others—landscape artists who sent their watercolors to engravers for translation. The

labels required a complex lithographic job, with a separate plate needed for each color. The result was fantastic—quality art on a very small scale. By the 1950s, when cardboard boxes replaced wooden crates, the label business ended. Stacks of abandoned labels, never used, found their way into the market. Today, there have been books written and museum exhibitions held about them, and they're highly collectible. Yet they're still one of the few attractive things you can buy under ten dollars!

# The Side Yard

**Total Cost: $1,284.45**

YOU DON'T HAVE TO USE YOUR YARD to get enjoyment out of it. Even if you have no time for sunning or barbecues, you can create a space you'll enjoy looking at from the inside. A chaise longue, table, chair, and sculpture base combine to make a satisfying vignette that evokes a mood of outdoor leisure.

I chose what at first might look like "odds and ends" for a couple of reasons. I didn't want a matching set of tables and chairs that screamed "patio furniture." Rather, I wanted to create a space that was an extension of the living/dining area. Using the same kind of furniture—wicker and distressed woods—did the trick. For example, I bought an outsized newel post and used it as a stand alongside the chaise longue. The chaise, upholstered with tropical barkcloth, was so attractive it didn't need changing. (I'd tried it in the master bedroom and in the loft before determining that it looked best in the side yard.)

## Costs: SIDE YARD

| | | |
|---|---|---:|
| 1. | Bamboo Vintage Chaise Longue | $699.50 |
| 2. | Wicker End Table | $39.95 |
| 3. | Newel Post from a porch, circa 1920 | $39.95 |
| 4. | White Wicker Chair, circa 1920 | $75.00 |
| 5. | French Country Lantern | $36.00 |
| 6. | Ralph Lauren Kennebunkport Fabric | $18.99 |
| | SUBTOTAL | $909.39 |
| | SHIPPING | $283.05 |
| | TRANSFORMATION (upholstery) | $92.01 |
| | TOTAL | $1,284.45 |

109

## assembling furniture

About 60 percent of everything sold on eBay
is new from manufacturers, retailers, and
jobbers who want to offload excess goods. As
many of these objects come in pieces in their
original boxes (NIB—new in box), you have
to assemble them. The Adirondack chair was
one. It was made of cypress and could be
ordered in a number of colors. I ordered it
in white to put outdoors, but later painted
it green and put it in the living room.

# The Powder Room

**Total Cost: $287.61**

I WAS INSPIRED TO LOOK at period photos by a friend, a curator of a West Coast museum. He organized a complete museum exhibition of Hollywood glamour photos by a lesser-known photographer—all purchased on eBay. That encouraged me to collect a few to lend a little 1930s glamour to the powder room. Instead of searching for certain photographers, I looked for particular stars, like Bette Davis and Jean Harlow. The best one I found was of Clark Gable, which I wound up giving to my mother, a lifelong fan. I painted the walls pale, silvery gray, which I thought would be an effective background for the photos. I tried to find some art deco–style embroidered guest towels but had no luck. On a whim, I did a search for "Frette" towels (the Rolls Royce of fine linen), and to my utter amazement, several lots came up. I can't wait for my towels at home to wear out, so I can upgrade and buy some Frette towels for myself!

### Costs: POWDER ROOM

| | |
|---|---:|
| Photo - Fred Astaire & Ginger Rogers Dancing | $5.99 |
| Photo - Jean Harlow | $19.99 |
| Photo - Bette Davis | $8.00 |
| Frette Towels | $31.55 |
| SUBTOTAL | $65.53 |
| SHIPPING | $11.00 |
| TRANSFORMATIONS (framing) | $211.08 |
| TOTAL | $287.61 |

# HALL TO THE POWDER ROOM:
# Handkerchief Hall

**Total Cost: $679.43**

DON'T GET ME STARTED on hankies. I've collected them for years, I've written two books on them, and I just plain love them. I'm not attracted to the delicate white lace squares women wear at their weddings. Rather, I prefer brighter bold ones, like the floral hankies from the 1940s and '50s in the hall. These hankies reflect the times in which they were made. During World War II, women entered the workforce in large numbers, and many became "Rosie the Riveter," holding down defense jobs formerly filled by men. As frightened as they were for their husbands, brothers, sons, and lovers who were in harm's way the world over, they made their own money and valued their independence. The hanky, which had gone out with the advent of Kleenex in the 1920s, came back as a fashion accessory, providing women with an easy fix for the urge to shop and an inexpensive way to keep their spirits up.

In my own house, I've framed hankies and hung them like paintings. The hall in the eBay house provided the opportunity to do the same. Since I was only going for a look, and not searching for "masterpieces" to add to my own collection, I didn't have to have the rarest, most expensive examples. The seller of the first one I bought e-mailed me to send payment to the LOST AND FOUND DEPOT of Fillmore, California. What ingenuity on the part of some city official! As I needed a dozen or so hankies, I soon realized it was quicker and a lot cheaper to buy several at a time. A lot of eighteen came up, which I bought for $19.99—less than what I've paid for some of the singles I own. When the package arrived, I was disappointed. Many of the eighteen were soiled (I don't remember the seller mentioning that), and others less attractive than they appeared in the photos. Once they were framed and hung on the walls, however, they looked splendid. It's all in the presentation: The effect was one of a giant still life—at a fraction of the cost.

| Costs: POWDER ROOM HALL | |
|---|---|
| Vintage Floral Handkerchiefs | $19.99 |
| SUBTOTAL | $19.99 |
| SHIPPING | $4.50 |
| TRANSFORMATION @ $59.54 each | $654.94 |
| TOTAL | $679.43 |

## framing handkerchiefs

Botanical prints are lovely, but you see them everywhere. I went for a framed bouquet of floral hankies in the hall leading to the guest bedroom. The frames cost more than the hankies, but the completed effect was well worth it.

# CHOOSING FRAMES

A good frame can make all the difference to the look of a room. It can give weight to an area that "needs something." An attractive frame can make an inexpensive poster, like the flamingo in the master bedroom (which cost close to $30), look like a million dollars. I took everything that I wanted to frame—posters, a Hawaiian shirt, photos, needlepoint, handkerchiefs, and a tablecloth—to Quick Frames. I probably could have gotten some of the smaller frames on eBay, but buying them all from the framer saved time, and the selection was better. A good framer is like a great chef who knows just what the dish needs to give it zing. What would have taken me hours on my own, took no time with the framer's advice. Choosing the mat that separates the frame from what's being framed isn't easy either. I tried, especially on the Pucci scarves in the girl's room, to use colorful mats, but in the end I preferred off-white every time.

There's the right frame for a work and a wrong one. Framers have hundreds of frame corners you can try against what you're framing to see which one looks best. For the needlepoints in the dining room and alcove, for example, dark frames, slightly stressed to look old, worked wonderfully. For the palm tree prints in the master bedroom, a lighter, airier frame was more in keeping with the cloudlike feeling of the room.

# The Guest Room

**Total Cost: $8,214.62**

GO FISH. My plan in creating a guest bedroom was to make visitors feel like they were on a vacation at an Adirondack fishing camp. The fishing tackle, Navajo rugs, Pendleton blankets, and decoys all conjure up lazy days near a mountain lake. I started by asking myself what Ralph Lauren would be looking at for inspiration if he were designing a new "Adirondack Collection." I did a search for "Adirondack," then "Yosemite," "Camp," and "Mountain Lodge." All turned up great things.

The bedside table lamps were a great find. I couldn't have imagined any more perfect for the room. They're made of logs and are typical of rustic, mountain-style furnishings (right). When city folk in the early twentieth century built mountain lodges for themselves, they tended to take whatever they could carry (usually small things) up to the mountains, and they'd make the big things, like lamps, tables, and chairs, out of whatever materials they could find there, such as logs. The lampshades were made from a blue-and-white ticking trimmed in a blue plaid.

My favorite object, which makes the room for me, is a small useless sign in the shape of a canoe—Camp-Run-a-Muck (opposite). It's all in the details.

After spending considerable time buying things for the room, I came to my senses. Why reinvent the wheel, when you can just buy Ralph Lauren? So I went back on eBay and searched for "Ralph Lauren." I got the blanket for the bed, the sheets, and pillowcases—all RL, all new in the package. They may have been last season's, but who cares? If imitation is the highest form of flattery, "Ralph, I love you."

## Costs: GUEST ROOM

| | |
|---|---|
| 1. Hickory Arm Chair | $412.00 |
| 2. Blanket Chest, circa 1840 | $300.00 |
| 3. Iron and Brass Bed | $247.50 |
| 4. Mission-Style Side Table | $239.99 |
| 5. Rustic Log Lamps (pair) | $56.01 |
| 6. Duck Decoys (7) | $481.50 |
| 7. Sock Monkeys (6) | $113.22 |
| 8. Tall, Cylindrical Adirondack Pack Basket | $149.00 |
| 9. Canoe Sign | $16.99 |
| 10. Feather Brand Canoe Paddles | $81.00 |
| 11. Canoe Paddles with bands of wood grains | $79.00 |
| 12. Ralph Lauren Bed Linens & Blanket | $304.78 |
| 13. Standard Pillows (4) | $29.98 |
| 14. Beacon Bathrobe | $47.00 |
| 15. Adirondack Picture Frame | $9.95 |
| 16. Folk Art Painting | $12.00 |
| 17. Arts and Crafts Copper Bowl | $45.00 |
| 18. Arts and Crafts Copper Vase | $45.00 |
| 19. Fabrics for Lampshades | $26.25 |
| 20. French Ticking Fabric for Drapes | $59.00 |
| Victorian Plant Stand (side table) | $175.00 |
| Camping and Fishing Gear | $766.15 |
| Indian Blankets (11) | $772.59 |
| Navajo Rugs (5) | $1,945.00 |
| Split Log Carry Basket | $24.99 |
| Display Canoe Paddle | $42.77 |
| **SUBTOTAL** | $6,481.67 |
| **SHIPPING** | $1,250.46 |
| **TRANSFORMATIONS** (lampshades and wiring, painting, framing) | $482.49 |
| **TOTAL** | $8,214.62 |

## the hickory chair

I love the hickory armchair. It embodied the rustic charm I wanted for the room. The chair cost $412, and the seller, who lived in Arkansas, apologized for the high cost of shipping. She asked if I knew a cheaper way. She warned me that it would be difficult to reach her by phone as she'd had her phone service turned off. Her daughter, it seems, had abused her long-distance phone privileges, and she had no choice. This personal note was characteristic of the eBay fraternity; what parent worldwide wouldn't empathize?

**decoys** Duck decoys were originally carved to lure water birds within a hunter's range. No one thought of them as art; they were crudely carved. Over the years, however, decoys have made their way from the pond to the parlor. With their glass eyes, finely delineated wings, and charming, colorful names—such as "Mason Yellow Legs," "Shorebird," "Bluebill," "Old Ontario Whistler," and "Redhead"— they've become prized collectibles. I placed the decoys on high shelves that I'd built around three sides of the room about two feet from the ceiling. The wall behind was painted a rich blue-green, which I chose to refer to the birds' natural habitat.

**navajo rugs** Although Navajo women had woven clothing and blankets for centuries, they only started making rugs when they came into contact with traders and realized how saleable they were. Navajo rugs are a collector's dream. The evolution of patterns and styles, which continues today, makes collecting contemporary Navajos as satisfying for some as collecting antique examples is for others. You can spend tens of thousands of dollars on a museum-quality Navajo or you can go on eBay and, for much less, find attractive bargains you can lay over a carpet, throw over the back of a sofa, or hang on the wall.

**blanket chest** Before I found this one, I bought another. The seller took my money, but never sent the chest. I didn't hear from him for a long while. After many harangues on my part, he e-mailed that he was returning my money. It was the end of the year, he explained, and the chest was in a storage bin, which he wanted to close out. He'd sold everything, including the chest, forgetting that I'd purchased it. Can't hate the guy for an honest mistake. It left me to scramble for another one. Luckily, I found another I liked better.

# Indian blankets

Unlike Navajo rugs, "Indian" blankets aren't Indian at all. They were made by Eastern woolen mills for sale to Indians at trading posts. Over time, they became popular throughout America, to the point that the names of certain mills, like Pendleton and Beacon, have become the generic term for these blankets. Thus, a "Pendleton blanket" or "Beacon blanket" could have been made by a dozen other mills. Today, older blankets are serious collectors' items, as only a few survive in good condition. I particularly like the bathrobe (below), which came in its original box (left).

# sock monkeys

I don't know why I like sock monkeys; I never played with them when I was a child. For years, I passed them up at flea markets, thinking they were a ragtag bunch. Then one day, a couple of years ago, my attitude changed. I went to a museum where over a thousand of them were on view. I had an epiphany. I had to have some, pronto. I nearly ran all the way home to get onto eBay to start searching. Usually, I take the time to learn and study a new area of interest, but that night, I recklessly plunged in.

Just as there are specialists in everything on the Internet, eBay is peopled with sock monkey enthusiasts who can date them, rate them, etc. It's two years since I bought my first, and I'm still no connoisseur. I don't care whether I have one of the first red-heeled monkeys made in the 1890s or not. I know very little about their history, except that women started making them from old athletic socks (and still do). I've learned to tell the difference between old and new ones, but frankly, I don't care. I'm indiscriminate; I love them all. I love them because each one has its own character. There are princess sock monkeys, baby sock monkeys, freaky sock monkeys, and dozens of other types—always with those big soulful eyes. I love these appealing, nutty dolls, and I'd like any house to have some. One sock monkey doesn't do it for me. I need a bunch of them. One is okay, but twelve is better, and twenty better still.

My search for sock monkeys led me to one of my nicest experiences on the Internet. Mistakenly, I paid twice for one. The seller, Sallysewsomuch, offered to return my $25 or to make another sock monkey to my specifications. I chose the sock monkey and encouraged her to make whatever she wanted. A few weeks later, a magnificent "queen" arrived, resplendent in a beaded crown, ruff, and flowing blue skirt. La Reina has become my favorite of all. The idea that I could commission a sock monkey sparked an idea. I asked Sallysewsomuch to make one of Bert, a lawyer. The sock monkey just arrived (below), dressed

like Bert—in a pinstripe suit, striped tie, and glasses—ready for court. I plan on giving it to Bert for his birthday. Can you keep it a secret?

| Costs: GUEST ROOM—SOCK MONKEYS | |
|---|---|
| 1. Sock monkey girl with gingham dress | $10.49 |
| 2. Sock monkey with strands of hair on top of head | $16.39 |
| 3. Sock monkey missing pompom on one foot | $15.50 |
| 4. Sock monkey with long eyelashes | $13.49 |
| 5. Sock monkey girl with socks and white pompoms | $36.65 |
| 6. Sock monkey wearing sweater with three pompoms | $20.70 |
| TOTAL | $113.22 |

# The Stairwell

**Total Cost: $413.45**

THE SURFBOARD WAS A LEAD-IN to what followed at the top of the stairs—the surfer/Polynesian-themed loft. I bought two surfboards, but it took only one to fill the space. The other hangs in my garage, where it makes me laugh every night when I pull in my car.

In Victorian times, there were thousands of butterfly collectors whose collections were more about the experience of the hunt than the specimens they gathered. They kept ledgers on the where and when of their captures, like plane spotters do today. Nowadays, making a butterfly collection is a lot easier; all you have to do is go on eBay, do a search for "butterflies" or "butterfly collection," and you have thousands to choose from. The three collections of butterflies I bought came framed and ready to hang.

| Costs: **THE STAIRWELL** | |
|---|---|
| 1. Viking Surfboard | $199.00 |
| 2. Painted Peruvian Butterfly Collection (18) | $41.00 |
| 3. Butterflies with Blue Morpho (13) | $35.00 |
| 4. Farm-Raised Butterfly Collection (6) | $32.00 |
| SUBTOTAL | $307.00 |
| SHIPPING | $106.45 |
| TOTAL | $413.45 |

SUNSHINE
beach boy

ADVANCE
RETAIL
TRADE
EDITION

HOLIDAY TRAVEL
RESORT FASHIONS

# The Tiki Room

**Total Cost: $6,156.00**

FOR CENTURIES, POLYNESIA has symbolized the exotic. Restaurant and bar owners recognized this early on, and by the middle of the twentieth century, Polynesian-themed restaurants and bars cropped up in cities and towns across America. Watering holes, such as Trader Vic's, Don the Beachcomber, and thousands of knock-offs delighted us as kids, with their tiki gods, palm frond entrances, and gardenia-laden fruit punch. Having been one of those kids, I decided to have some tiki-based fun in my eBay house. So I typed in "Polynesian," "Hawaiian," "Island," and off I went.

One night I typed in "tiki bar" and started scrolling down. Heavens, so many are so kitsch—with raffia skirts or carved masks on the fronts. I quickly found one that was no frills. If a tiki bar could be elegant, this was it. Still, I wanted to scroll through the listings to make sure there wasn't one I liked better. As I've said, one of the great things about eBay is that it's like going to hundreds of shops to do comparative shopping—without worrying about traffic, parking, or getting home on time for dinner.

The furniture in this room is a mixture of standard island stuff, like the tiki bar, and high-design items. The sofa, side tables, and the tiki bar are made of rattan. The coffee table is a restrike of a Noguchi (according to the seller), and the 1950s lamps are probably by Paul Frankl, a well-known West Coast architect/designer ($125). The red lampshades add even more drama to an already high-drama room.

## Costs: TIKI ROOM

| | | |
|---|---|---:|
| 1. | Tiki Bar from 1950s | $649.50 |
| 2. | Rattan Sofa, Loveseat, & Chair | $199.00 |
| 3. | Noguchi Coffee Table | $489.00 |
| 4. | Orange Herman Miller Shell Chair | $222.50 |
| 5. | Wicker End Tables (2) | $81.00 |
| 6. | Rattan Magazine Rack | $51.00 |
| 7. | Vinyl Records (25) | $370.60 |
| 8. | Surfing Photos | $85.00 |
| 9. | Vintage Radios (5) | $265.38 |
| 10. | Frankl Bamboo Lamps (2) | $125.00 |
| 11. | Lava Lamp | $12.50 |
| 12. | Electric Fan | $12.51 |
| 13. | Vintage Ukulele | $124.50 |
| 14. | Fly to Hawaii Poster | $14.99 |
| 15. | Seashells | $77.47 |
| 16. | Art Pottery Matte Green Dish | $26.00 |
| 17. | Barkcloth Drapes & Other Fabrics for Upholstery and Pillows | $585.00 |
| | Hawaii Territory Map 1930 | $6.00 |
| | Hawaii Pan Am Poster | $22.99 |
| | Vintage Shirt with Surfboard Print | $31.00 |
| | "Surfing History" - Miniature Surfboards | $68.00 |
| | Beach Boys Sheet Music / Photos | $19.98 |

| | |
|---|---:|
| SUBTOTAL | $3,538.92 |
| SHIPPING | $811.39 |
| TRANSFORMATIONS (upholstery, pillows, lampshades, framing) | $1,805.69 |
| TOTAL | $6,156.00 |

## Hawaiian shirt

Years ago, I had a bad eBay experience buying a vintage Hawaiian shirt. My husband collects them, and I bid on one described as "vintage." When it arrived, it wasn't vintage at all. It looked old, but that's because it had been washed a lot. I couldn't be certain that I was being defrauded though; perhaps the seller didn't know the difference. I gave him the benefit of the doubt and said nothing. Bert wears it to walk the dogs. They don't care. So I was understandably wary when I went on eBay again to find one for the tiki room. What I found was perfect—a shirt with a surfboard pattern. It wasn't vintage, and I wasn't worried about fit, so the pressure was off. I became nervous only when the vendor asked me to route all correspondence through his friend, "cherietheglitterbug." He said that there was a hurricane and power outage in southeast Virginia, where he lived. When the shirt finally arrived, I was relieved: It was everything I'd hoped it would be.

## Noguchi coffee table

Repros are attractive, but don't pay the price of an original. Again, it's hard to tell from a thumbnail photo on eBay. The black-based Noguchi coffee table I bought for the tiki loft cost about half of what originals go for. Either I was getting an original in poor condition or it was a repro. The seller said he didn't know, and I made the deal. I wanted it either way.

## orange chair

The seller of the orange chair was covering all his bases when he described it as being "Charles Eames, Herman Miller, Knoll style." I bought it despite his odd stream of consciousness: "Well, when Mable's ass went to sleep, Jimmy had to go upstairs to the accounting firm to get a chair. While he was coming back he must have fallen on top of the chair and rode the thing down. Thank goodness for the shaggy rugs of the '80s. The chair got no other real scratches on it except some fairly minor bruises." Mabel's ass? The "accounting firm upstairs" in his home? Or in an office building with no elevator but stairs covered with "shaggy rugs"? Beats me. Later, I got another confessional e-mail, "Yikes—last night I did notice that this crack yawns a bit when you torque around in the chair, lean back, push out on the armrest." And then, there was the part about shipping. "Worldwide shipping also available, like to Japan is about $175." I meant to e-mail him back with assurances that he needn't worry: I wouldn't be torquing my way to Japan in the chair any time soon!

**vinyl records** A wall of colored records reads like an op art painting from the 1960s. Deciding on which to buy only had to do with color. Therefore, I felt guilty when a knowledgeable seller admitted sadly that the yellow vinyl I'd bought from him—an original 1957 Fran Warren album that included the song "Come Rain or Come Shine," in perfect condition—was stolen from his car before he could ship it to me. He'd stopped at the hospital to visit a sick friend, and the car, with my record in it, had been ransacked. He offered me another, with scratches, along with a partial refund. It was hard to work up the nerve to admit to such a maven that I'd only bought the record to hang on the wall. He sent me the duplicate with scratches, I got a reduction, and everyone was happy. Whenever you hang anything on the wall, put a piece of transparent tape on the wall before hammering in a nail or hook. That way, the plaster and paint won't chip beyond what's absolutely necessary.

**electric fan** The vintage oscillating fan was made by Superior Electric Production Corporation. Honesty rules. I never would have known I'd made the mistake of paying twice for it, but the seller e-mailed me that I should be on the lookout; he'd attached the second check to the package.

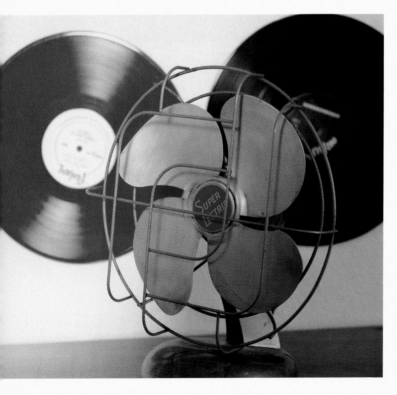

## plastic radios

In *The Graduate*, an older man whispers to Dustin Hoffman the one-word secret of success—"plastics." Maybe he was right. In the decades after plastics were invented, they became the material of choice for numerous household appliances, including radios. Today, when radio collectors get together, they debate the qualities of the different kinds of early plastic—from Bakelite (which came in only black or brown), to Plaskon, Catalin, and Beetle (which came in vivid colors). I chose the radios strictly for color, to play off the tropical fabrics and the vinyl records.

# The Boy's Room

**Total Cost: $2,803.23**

DECORATING A ROOM for a growing boy isn't easy. What could be cool enough for a nine-year-old? *Star Wars*? Cowboys and Indians? Whatever it is today, it'll change next year. eBay gives you the confidence to go all out, because you can sell the cowboy bunk bed on eBay when the kid wants something else. Sure, you could lose a little money, but you might even make some.

I decided to go with sports, model airplanes, and motorcycles. Whatever furniture I bought had to be "indestructible." What better than metal to take a beating? I've always wanted a locker at home like those we had at school. For a boy, throwing all his things into a locker is an easy way of keeping the room neat. The metal table probably came from a hospital. A dealer in vintage metal furniture with the moniker "heartvintagesteel," whose specialty is refinishing old pieces, sold me the swivel chair. I was delighted that he gave me a choice of color for the seat cushion.

The four walls are painted different colors— taken from the camouflage fabric used for the drapes and pillows. Before you paint, don't forget to cover the moldings with painters' tape and the floor with plastic to protect from dripping!

149

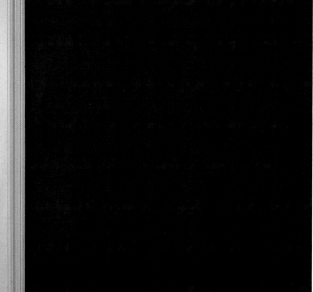

## Costs: BOY'S ROOM

| | | |
|---|---|---:|
| 1. | Office Desk Chair | $395.00 |
| 2. | Metal Bookcase | $299.00 |
| 3. | Locker | $137.00 |
| 4. | Metal Scooter Pre-WWII | $90.00 |
| 5. | WWI & WWII Airplane Posters | $48.90 |
| 6. | Model Airplanes (2) | $146.99 |
| 7. | Camouflage Fabrics | $234.09 |
| 8. | Sports Equipment | $75.49 |
| 9. | World Globe | $11.50 |
| 10. | Ralph Lauren Sheets & Blanket | $110.19 |
| | Medicine Cabinet | $75.00 |
| | Mission-Style Plant Stand | $599.99 |
| | Brass Desk Lamp | $29.95 |
| | Photo - WWII Plane and Crew | $9.00 |
| | Army Flashlight | $9.99 |
| | Standard Pillows (2) | $14.99 |

| | |
|---|---:|
| SUBTOTAL | $2,287.08 |
| SHIPPING | $424.29 |
| TRANSFORMATIONS (painting, framing) | $91.86 |
| TOTAL | $2,803.23 |

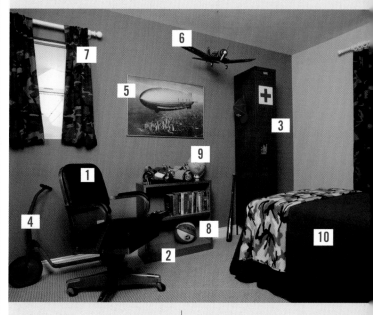

**scooter** I received the following e-mail, obviously from a grown-up daughter: "My parents are leaving for their winter trip tomorrow, and they were wondering if you've received the scooter yet." Do you think the writer was having an anxiety attack at the loss of a favorite childhood toy?

**camouflage fabric** The camouflage fabric (opposite) was so delightful that I e-mailed the vendor asking for more—enough to cover one of the walls and make curtains. She replied that she had the same pattern in "Taffida." I thought that was some kind of trademark, until I realized that it was "taffeta" misspelled. She created a listing, I bid on it and bought it, but, in the end, it was too flimsy to use. But, hey, camouflage taffeta? That's unique!

# The Girl's Room

**Total Cost: $3,630.40**

MY GOAL WAS TO CREATE a room overflowing with the exuberance of a teenage girl. Teens need their own space, and this one, with giant graphics on the wall, is not for the faint of heart.

Most teenage girls are interested in clothes, so I tried to combine fashion and design. Often, young girls are drawn to pink and purple, so I chose those colors in an incarnation of a Pucci design from the 1960s (overleaf). A favorite of the Jackie O jet set, Emilio Pucci made bold, colorful designs that are popular all over again. A hot pink shag rug, a lava lamp, and some '60s-style furniture completed the look. Some pieces are old, but most are recent copies, like the boomerang tables called "Eames Knoll era" by the seller ($68 for two). Nonetheless, they're great.

Why not make Pucci scarves the theme of the room? Finding vintage examples on eBay proved impossible, so I settled for new ones. With eBay, there's always the chance you'll find some, but I had no luck at the time. I framed three scarves and made another into a pillow. Like Pucci, who signed his prints, all of us who painted the wall signed our names. Does that make us "taggers"? I like the fact that my close friend Lucrecia helped me; the first Pucci dress I ever saw was on her in the 1960s. Each of the other walls was painted a different color, also taken from the Pucci scarf. Maybe I went a little overboard, but I love it.

**desk chair** A restrike by Vitra of Verner Panton's famous "Panton chair" came NIB. The first single-molded plastic chair designed by Panton dates from 1967.

**endless summer poster** This poster was designed by a California college art student in 1964 for *The Endless Summer*, the groundbreaking film on surfing. The student was paid only $150 for his design, and the poster, like the film, has become a cult item.

## Costs: GIRL'S ROOM

| | | |
|---|---|---:|
| 1. | White Ball "Pastil" Chair by Eero Aarnio | $725.00 |
| 2. | White Molded Plastic Chair by Verner Panton | $199.00 |
| 3. | Isamu Noguchi Cylinder Lamps (2) | $300.00 |
| 4. | Boomerang Bedside Tables (2) | $68.00 |
| 5. | Hot Pink Shag Rug | $120.00 |
| 6. | Pucci Scarves & Fabric | $212.99 |
| 7. | Orange Pashmina | $16.99 |
| 8. | Standard Pillows (2) | $14.99 |
| 9. | Bed Linens - Orange and Purple Spread | $70.26 |
| 10. | Fabric for Drapes and Giant Cushion | $44.99 |
| | Iron/ Wood/ Laminate 1950s Desk | $280.55 |
| | Small White Circular Knoll Table by Eero Saarinen | $300.00 |
| | Pink Glitter Lava Lamp | $12.50 |
| | George Nelson Ball Clock | $165.00 |
| | Ericofon Phone | $160.30 |
| | Electric Guitar and Stand | $112.98 |
| | Freeform Mobile, 1950s | $32.50 |
| | Endless Summer Poster | $18.99 |
| | **SUBTOTAL** | **$2,855.04** |
| | SHIPPING | $618.32 |
| | TRANSFORMATIONS (pillows, frames) | $157.04 |
| | **TOTAL** | **$3,630.40** |

## lava lamp and telephone (this page, left) The Ericofon, invented
in Sweden, was one of the greatest innovations in telephone design—a one-piece phone.
Brought to market in the mid-1950s, for use in hospitals, it became an instant success in
Europe. Although Americans loved it (and it was available in eighteen colors), Bell Telephone,
with its monopoly hold, never let it really catch on. In its heyday in the 1960s, the lava lamp
connoted a marijuana, hippie culture. Now, it's risen to be a perennial in décor.

## ball chair In their enthusiasm, many sellers who don't know what they have
call their pieces by as many names as they can think of. MOD AARNIO EAMES PANTON
JOE COLOMBO were names all strung together as a title for the listing of this fiberglass
ball-shaped chair (a restrike of a chair designed by Eero Aarnio and produced in Finland).
Its name, the Pastil chair, is a corruption of the French word for "small candy." The
imaginative seller enthusiastically claimed that the chair was inspired by an astronaut's
helmet. I'd never heard that before, but, hey, I bought it. Why not? The vendor brought
attention to the chair's versatility, adding, "In summer it is big fun to sit in the chair
floating on water, in winter gliding down a small hill with speed." Quite a tall order
for a chair!

## midcentury modern furniture

When you move into a new house or apartment, it's natural to want to buy new furniture. If you do—a chair here, a table there—it quickly adds up. Later, if you want to sell, ouch! New furniture has little or no resale value. Because good antiques and vintage furniture are readily saleable, often at a profit, you might consider buying some of those. English or French eighteenth- or nineteenth-century furniture is great, but not everyone has a house where it would fit, and/or the money to buy it. For those who prefer contemporary furniture, midcentury modern is a good bet.

I started buying midcentury modern furniture because I associated it with my mother. In one day, she got rid of all our dark colonial-style furniture, painted the walls white, and installed blond wood modern pieces. Who knew? I had a Swedish modern mother!

Pieces by 1950s and '60s designers, like Isamu Noguchi and George Nelson, were superbly designed even though mass-produced. For this reason, they can cost just a little more than furniture at the Pottery Barn or Crate and Barrel. Prime examples are sought after by museums and savvy collectors. This is one instance when you can afford to own a chair just like one you'd find in the Museum of Modern Art.

## Noguchi lamp (right)

This Isamu Noguchi "cylinder lamp," circa 1944, was originally designed for his sister in aluminum and manufactured by Knoll in 1944. I placed these paper-and-wood reproductions on a pair of boomerang bedside tables.

**clock** The ball clock was designed by George Nelson in 1948. The one I bought came NIB and was described by the seller as an " 'authentic' authorized re-edition," whatever that means.

## Pucci-inspired wall

The wall colors in the girl's room—lime green, hot pink, and mulberry—come from a Pucci scarf I framed and hung above the bed. A blown-up version of the scarf, a kind of super-graphic, covers an entire wall. You can do this by drawing the arcs with a pencil attached to a long string and then painting in the spaces. Looking for an activity to get the family in on the act? This is it! It took half a day and a handful of friends, and it was great fun. We all signed our names as Emilio Pucci had done on his scarves.

# The Kids' Bathroom

**Total Cost: $344.26**

EVERY ROOM SHOULD HAVE its own collection, and the kids' bathroom should be no exception. If you choose objects that fit with the room, all the better. Just as the kitchen has its orange crate labels, what better way to decorate a bathroom than with a collection of toothbrush holders?

I've collected vintage toothbrush holders for years now and love them. In the eBay house, I placed them on a high shelf built all around the room, a foot down from the ceiling. Again, I could forgo the real collectors' examples and get away with buying newer, inexpensive ones. Here again, eBay rules. At an antique show or flea market, I'd be lucky to find one. eBay offers dozens every day.

**Bert's genie** A powerful presence guards my husband's bathroom—a green-turbaned genie in an orange cloak (left), his arms folded as if to say "go no farther." Fortunately, he's made of pottery, and, from turban to toe, he's only six inches high. In the crook of each arm, he holds a toothbrush. He's the first toothbrush holder I'd ever seen. If you're not familiar with toothbrush holders, I recommend that you look at them on eBay. They're colorful, amusing, and widely varied companions. Every time I brush my teeth, I look at them and giggle. If they were less cute, I probably wouldn't brush my teeth as often as I do.

## Cost: CHILDREN'S BATHROOM

Toothbrush Holders:

| | | |
|---|---|---|
| 1. | Dachshund Dog Cup | $11.00 |
| 2. | White Cow with Black Spots | $1.99 |
| 3. | Lady with Big Skirt and Hat | $16.60 |
| 4. | Winnie the Pooh | $3.70 |
| | Happy Lips | $1.99 |
| | Cat & Mouse | $3.00 |
| | Bugs Bunny | $3.00 |
| | Plaid Rabbit | $4.00 |
| | Striped Cat | $4.00 |
| | Pink Elephant | $4.99 |
| | Green Frog | $5.98 |
| | Snowman | $6.99 |
| | Donald Duck | $7.92 |
| | Fat Pig | $10.50 |
| | Daffy Duck | $11.51 |
| | Bee Hive | $12.51 |
| | Cowboy Saddle | $15.95 |
| | Swan | $16.25 |
| | Yellow Baby Duckling | $1.99 |
| | Snoopy Flying Ace | $33.30 |
| | White and Black Cow | $3.00 |
| | Toothbrushes | $9.99 |
| | Blue Towels | $35.91 |
| | SUBTOTAL | $226.07 |
| | SHIPPING | $118.19 |
| | TOTAL | $344.26 |

# The Laundry Room

**Total Cost: $131.66**

HAVING A SPACIOUS, light-filled laundry is a luxury. The challenge was to make it a full-fledged, attractive room on its own and not just an appliance-filled closet. I made the curtains out of a remnant of blue-and-white gingham. Finally, I hung Shaker-style pegs on the left wall. They're not only decorative, but also provide a great way to hang a small collection of vintage laundry bags. Although they're inexpensive, they're so good-looking, you'd never want to use them for your dirty socks and underwear!

I started by painting the far wall of the laundry room blue-and-white plaid. I did it the way Doug Funkhouser taught me, by laying down painters' masking tape on the blue wall and stippling the in-between spaces with white paint on a rag. I hadn't realized how proprietary I felt about the house until then. As I painted, knowing how much my husband hates plaid, I started feeling guilty. Only then did I stop to realize that this wasn't his house at all—or mine!

## Costs: LAUNDRY ROOM

| | |
|---|---:|
| 1. Scottie Dog Laundry Bag | $32.02 |
| 2. Basket Laundry Bag | $10.99 |
| 3. Embroidery Laundry Bag | $19.05 |
| 4. Butterfly Laundry Bag | $5.51 |
| 5. Blue & White Gingham Fabric | $31.00 |
| 6. Peg Rack | $12.50 |
| SUBTOTAL | $111.07 |
| SHIPPING | $20.59 |
| TOTAL | $131.66 |

# The Master Suite

Total Cost: **$12,424.87**

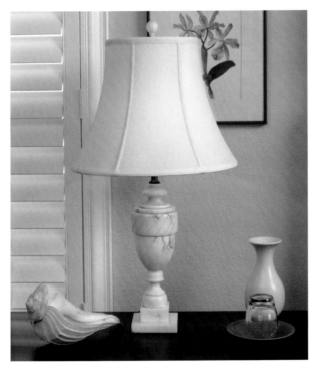

WITH CELL PHONES, pagers, carpools, and kids, it's hard for a couple to find time to be alone. That's why their bedroom should be an oasis of peace and privacy. A creamy palette, antique furniture, soft-glow lamps, embroidered pillowcases, and Persian rugs all contribute to the room's atmosphere of luxurious calm. To these, I added a touch of the British Colonial with a Raffles four-poster bed and a ceiling fan lazily turning overhead (overleaf).

It's hard to create a bedroom in which both a man and a woman would be comfortable. Many women have a fantasy of voile and lace, while men usually prefer something more masculine. Here, I tried to combine things that would please both—the dark wood is masculine and the beiges and white are soft enough to please any woman.

**chaise longue** When I realized the master bedroom was big enough to accommodate my fantasy chaise longue, I tried my luck finding one. I found a marvelous example. The seller called it a walnut "fainting chaise from the 1880s," and asked bidders to recognize that such a "genuine article . . . steady, stable . . . can be laid on with no problem. . . ." It was the second most expensive object I bought ($1,695). The fabric cost $285 and the cost for reupholstery was $475. The total came to $2,455. Gulp! Expensive, but why shouldn't someone splurge for one of the most important pieces of furniture in the house? Besides, it's a major design element in the room and can be seen from the top of the stairs.

## prints

I bought posters and inexpensive reproductions—all of palms, botanical specimens, and maps—for a few dollars each. What I didn't know was that some of the vendors had ripped pages out of books. I would never have bought them if I'd known. The next time, I'll ask before buying. The "Audubon" flamingo poster was the most expensive by a mile at $28.50. I doubt that anyone walking through the room would know that this wasn't an original Audubon. If authentic, by the way, it would cost around $200,000.

## Costs: MASTER SUITE

| | | |
|---|---|---:|
| 1. | Victorian Chaise Longue | $1,695.00 |
| 2. | Raffles Bed | $1,295.00 |
| 3. | Plantation Armchair | $219.95 |
| 4. | Settee at Base of Bed | $66.00 |
| 5. | Alabaster Lamps (3) | $182.00 |
| 6. | Jaipour Rug | $202.50 |
| 7. | Sarouk Rug | $171.74 |
| 8. | Chinese and Korean Pottery Bowls | $133.88 |
| 9. | Assorted Seashells | $89.94 |
| 10. | White Matelasse Coverlets for Chaise Upholstery & Bed | $462.98 |
| 11. | Antique Pillow Cases | $43.99 |
| 12. | Beige Pashmina | $22.50 |
| 13. | Gold Palm Tree and Other Fabric | $21.98 |
| 14. | Bed Linens and Pillows | $205.96 |
| 15. | Prints and Posters | $321.15 |
| 16. | Chippendale Game Table | $685.00 |
| | Empire Desk/Chest | $1,150.00 |
| | Empire Hat Rack | $685.00 |
| | Empire Chest of Drawers | $349.99 |
| | Victorian Demilune Console | $245.00 |
| | Pewter Aladdin Lamp | $79.99 |
| | Vintage San Francisco Map | $15.51 |
| | Grape Carved Corbels (2) | $100.00 |
| | Mirror with Woven Frame | $97.46 |
| | Ironstone Pitcher and Bowl | $90.01 |
| | Hurricane Candle Shades | $30.49 |
| | Faux Shagreen Box with Bone Inlay Border | $107.50 |
| | Burl Walnut Box | $48.00 |
| | Mother of Pearl Jewelry Box | $55.00 |

| | |
|---|---:|
| SUBTOTAL | $8,873.52 |
| SHIPPING | $1,899.45 |
| TRANSFORMATIONS (upholstery, pillows, framing, lampshades and wiring) | $1,651.90 |
| TOTAL | $12,424.87 |

## the bed

The bed was the first object in the house I looked for on eBay and just about the last I found. I was sure of what I wanted—a dark four-poster. I just couldn't find it. I searched for months under "Plantation," "Bermuda," "Colonial," "Malabar," "India," and "Mahogany." Out of desperation, I even tried "Sumatra." Along the way, I did buy an antique mahogany American Colonial style headboard, but it came broken, so I had to start from scratch. I finally found a "Raffles bed," named after the famous nineteenth-century Singapore hotel. Any Brit of social standing who traveled to Singapore at the time would have stayed at Raffles, named after the city's founder, Sir Stamford Raffles. It seemed to me that the bed embodied just what I was striving for—British elegance of the Colonial period. Eureka! It was the third most expensive object I bought for the house ($1,295). The online description said this hand-carved, hand-rubbed bed was made in India but was located in Colorado. What I didn't know until I bought it was that the bed was still in India. (May I suggest yet again that you "Do as I say and not as I do," and ask the vendor lots of questions before you bid?) A few weeks passed, and the bed still didn't arrive. There were only three weeks left before I was due to install everything in the Valencia house. I panicked and started nagging the vendor. The bed finally arrived in the United States—at the wrong port—and created a paperwork nightmare. Had I not been a pest, the bed would probably still be in shipping limbo. But it was worth it.

## bed linens

I particularly love antique linen pillow shams. It's amazing that antique textiles like the shams and the coverlet used to upholster the chaise longue are readily available at very low prices.

## plantation chair

The plantation chair (opposite left), was
one of the first things I bought on eBay.
Making a small pillow out of extra
barkcloth fabric added a sense of detail I
wanted to project. Although the chair is
new, it mixes well with the bedside tables,
the hat rack, and the chest, which are old,
if not antiques.

## captain's desk

The seller called this antique a work chest
(opposite right). I call it a captain's desk
because Bert has a similar one in his
office, and that's what he's always called
it. He says sea captains used these small
desks to keep and store their logs and
letters (closed top). Who knows? Even
though the seller told me he'd replaced the
leather top with vinyl, I bid on the piece
and got it. It wasn't cheap, but it added a
lot of class to the room.

## chest of drawers

The seller described the chest (right) as an
"antique Burl walnut chest of drawers . . .
dating to the mid-1800s." I'm not sure he
was accurate, but it was nonetheless worth
pursuing. The seller said he was starting
at a low number because he was moving
his store. I paid $349.99. Love the knobs!

# upholstery

Upholstery can be a costly transformation, but it adds immeasurably. Sometimes, as for the sofa and chair in the loft, I only had to have slipcovers made. Other times, as with the chaise longue in the master bedroom (this spread), the stuffing was lumpy and had to be redone. I tried print barkcloth first, but opted for white. A mattress-style seat cushion for the alcove in the living room was made using three different fabrics on the top, sides, and bottom. I unified a group of diverse dining chairs by using the same fabrics for all the seat cushions. The bar stools, with rush seats, didn't really need cushions, but covering them with the same fabric as the dining chairs linked the dining and kitchen areas aesthetically.

# The Master Bathroom

**Total Costs: $985.55**

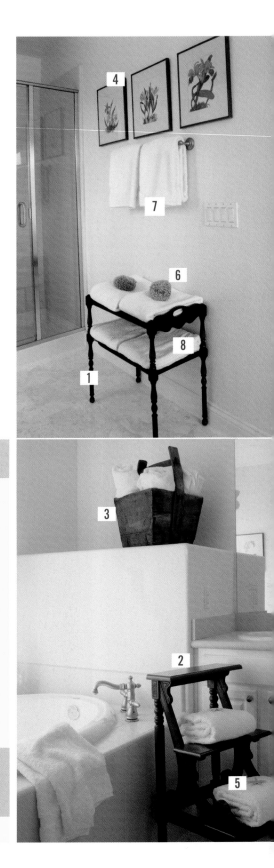

CARRYING THE THEME and colors of the master bedroom—dark furniture and creamy everything else—into the master bath led me to buy a two-tiered mahogany table, a Japanese wooden basket, and library steps. I rolled towels and stood them up in the basket, which turned out to be an appealing way to store them. The library steps and the table are perfect for storing towels as well.

## Costs: **MASTER BATHROOM**

| | | |
|---|---|---:|
| 1. | Mahogany Serving Table | $56.75 |
| 2. | Library Steps | $125.00 |
| 3. | Wooden Grain Bucket | $59.00 |
| 4. | Orchid Prints | $20.05 |
| 5. | Philippine Starfish | $26.00 |
| 6. | Natural Wool Sea Sponges | $21.00 |
| 7. | Frette Towels | $86.55 |
| 8. | White Bath Towels | $64.80 |
| | Palm Tree Print | $23.00 |
| | Celadon Ceramic Bowls | $29.66 |
| | Hurricane Candle Shade | $4.99 |
| | SUBTOTAL | $516.80 |
| | SHIPPING | $214.38 |
| | TRANSFORMATION (Framing) | $254.37 |
| | TOTAL | $985.55 |

# III. DECORATING
# WITH COLLECTIONS

**A GROUPING OF** similar objects is often far more interesting than one object by itself. Retailers know this; that's why they pile up boxes of Barbie dolls, makeup, or sunglasses. I found this to be true in the eBay house as well. One green pot, sock monkey, hanky, or ironstone plate by itself was nothing special. But a number of them grouped together . . . wow!!

I wanted it to seem as though the inhabitants of this house had been collecting over their lifetime, and eBay made it a breeze. "Collectibles" is eBay's biggest and most popular category. There are over a million and a half items on the block at any time, so it ended up being easy to create a collection of almost anything I wanted in a few weeks.

**Fiestaware** By the time I bought the Fiestaware (top left), I knew to go straight to the repros at a tenth of the price of an original.

**candlesticks** There are some collections I don't really consider collections at all (center left). I bought a lot of candlesticks, and Chinese bowls, for instance, without thinking of a greater whole. I just planned on using them to accessorize various rooms.

When I e-mailed the seller of a pair of glass candlesticks, asking what form of payment she preferred, she took it to mean I was having trouble paying. She kindly replied that she didn't need the money right then, and that I could pay whenever manageable. People like that lovely lady have kept me glued to eBay, long after the Valencia house was furnished and decorated.

**seashells** Shells and starfish are an inexpensive way to create an aura of natural relaxation, so I scattered them throughout the house (bottom left). They conjure up memories of a peaceful day seaside. Obviously, your purchases are impacted by where you live. If you live in the Florida Keys, you don't need to buy shells; you can pick them up on the beach. If you live in Nebraska, you can't do that.

## hurricane shades and corbels
When I put all the hurricane shades I bought together on one table, I was astonished at how terrific and glittery they looked. I placed them on architectural corbels (right) in a few spots in the house. I very much wanted to enrich the house with sculptural elements like these, which provided character by breaking the flat planes of the walls.

# Cheap and Cheaper

WHEREAS PASSIONATE COLLECTORS try to acquire objects that are rare and in perfect condition, that couldn't be a consideration when it came to the eBay house. My budget seldom left room for the best (or even nearly the best), so I had to find objects that were either authentic but blemished (and therefore cheaper) or "look-alikes" that generated the same feeling at a fraction of the price. Whether it was the midcentury furniture, Fiestaware, prints, majolica, toothbrush holders, or arts and crafts pottery, I may have compromised in terms of connoisseurship, but not in general appearance.

## arts and crafts vase

Sometimes, I started out without knowing my limits. I bought an Arts and Crafts vase for $272 that the seller, not sure what he had, called "Roseville Owens Teco Weller." Then I bought a poppy vase called "Arts and Crafts" for $112 and an Ephraim pottery pine cone vase for $155. Some quick math told me that I'd blow through my budget in no time if I kept buying on that level. So I had to come down to earth and buy less expensive examples. When I put them all together, the cheaper ones look more expensive placed among the good ones. The whole is worth more than the sum of its parts.

## toothbrush holders

You'd think I'd learn my lesson, but I did the same thing when it came to toothbrush holders: I bought a Snoopy Ace for $33.30. After that, I tried to keep my budget to under $20 for each. This one with Winnie the Pooh was $3.70.

# If Not a Painting, What?

YOU CAN FIND ALMOST ANYTHING you want on eBay—except really great or even good examples of fine art. Getting quality paintings that would work in the house and fit the budget proved very difficult. Yes, there were plenty of glow-in-the-dark nudes on black velvet, but a moderately priced, usable work by a competent professional seldom came up. I was afraid to use too many repros, photos, and posters, so I had to find alternatives in keeping with the spirit of each room.

## grouping varied shapes
As an art consultant, I'm used to the problem of the wall behind the sofa (left) crying out for art. I couldn't find a big painting I liked on eBay, so I thought the biggest painting I could find, a narrow horizontal still life, grouped with other objects, was the answer. But what kind of objects? That's where the fun began. I chose for shape—a long, skinny painting, a round mirror, a rectangular stained glass window—which all together created quite a dynamic composition.

## mirrors
A grouping of small mirrors in interesting frames (right) can easily take the place of a painting. It doesn't matter how fine any particular frame is; viewers take in and read the installation as a whole.

# Creating a Still Life

I WISH I WERE A STILL-LIFE PAINTER, but I haven't got the talent. I try to think like one, though, when I'm arranging furniture and objects on a table or a wall. That approach has enabled me to think differently about every room. Every table, every wall, and every corner provides an opportunity to create a marvelous still life—even the bathroom and laundry room.

I tried to think that way when I was buying things on eBay. What could I put on the coffee table? Stacks of books, a tea set, and a basket of lemons seemed to work. Hydrangeas, a birdhouse, and a sundial on a sofa side table (opposite). The potential for vignettes through the house kept my mind working and my fingers typing in bids. In the end, when it came to setting things out, trial and error taught me that an odd number of objects on a table work better than an even number. So when you're arranging elements, you might keep in mind: Three is better than two, five is better than four.

## the unexpected: dried flowers

It never occurred to me that flowers could be bought on eBay, so when I started searching, I did it as a lark. You can't imagine my excitement to find my favorite flower, the hydrangea, listed!

194

## the unexpected: vintage radios

What could be better on a Saturday afternoon than listening to golden oldies on a radio that was produced in the same era as the songs? A ukelele and some vintage books and magazines add to the experience. All you need is a Polynesian mai tai.